CISTERCIAN FATHERS SERIES: NUMBER TWELVE

WILLIAM OF ST THIERRY

Volume Four

THE GOLDEN EPISTLE

CISTERCIAN FATHERS SERIES: NUMBER TWELVE

THE WORKS OF
WILLIAM OF ST THIERRY

The Golden Fr tle

A Letter to the Brethren a

translated by
Theodore Berkeley OCSO

introduction by
J. M. Déchanet OSB

CISTERCIAN PUBLICATIONS, INC.
Kalamazoo, Michigan 49008

1980

Original Latin title: *Epistola [aurea] ad fratres de Monte-Dei*

ISBN 0-87907-712-3

Library of Congress Catalogue Card Number: 72-152482

© Cistercian Publications, Inc., 1971
THIRD PRINTING

Ecclesiastical permission to publish this book was received from
Bernard Flanagan, Bishop of Worcester, 13 July 1970.

Cistercian Publications, Inc.
WMU Station
Kalamazoo, Michigan 49008

Available in Britain and the Commonwealth through

A. R. Mowbray & Co Ltd
St Thomas House Becket Street
Oxford OX1 1SJ

Printed in the United States of America

CONTENTS

ABBREVIATIONS

Apo   Bernard of Clairvaux, *Cistercians and Cluniacs: St Bernard's Apology to Abbot William*, CF 1:33–69.

CF   Cistercian Fathers Series.

CG   William of St Thierry, *On Contemplating God*, CF 3:36–64.

EF   William of St Thierry, *Enigma of Faith*, CF 9.

Exp   William of St Thierry, *Exposition on the Song of Songs*, CF 6.

LBJ   *The Letters of St Bernard of Clairvaux*, trans. B. S. James (London: Burns and Oates, 1953).

LSB   *Vita Prima Bernardi*, trans. G. Webb and A. Walker, *St Bernard of Clairvaux* (Westminster, Md.: Newman, 1960).

Med   William of St Thierry, *Meditations*, CF 3:89–190.

MF   William of St Thierry, *The Mirror of Faith*, CF 9.

NBS   William of St Thierry, *On the Nature of Body and Soul*, CF 24.

NDL   William of St Thierry, *The Nature and Dignity of Love*, CF 15.

RB   *St Benedict's Rule for Monasteries*

Abbreviations for the Books of the Bible are taken from the Revised Standard Version.

INTRODUCTION

THE SPIRITUALITY OF WILLIAM OF ST
THIERRY was expressed both so perfectly and so practi-
cally in the *Epistle to the Brothers of Mont Dieu*, or the *Golden
Epistle*, that this alone of his many theological and mystical treatises
has held posterity's attention to any considerable extent. But, by
an ironical chance, it is under St Bernard's name that it has made
its triumphal progress through history. The first question that
arises in connection with William's spirituality can therefore be
summarized as: Bernard or William?—William or Bernard?

The first aim of this study must be to get rid of an equivocation
before solving a problem.[1]

The History of the Golden Epistle

The substitution of St Bernard's name for William's, at the beginning of the *Golden Epistle*, goes back to the second half of the
twelfth century, a few years after it had been sent to the Carthusians
of Mont Dieu.[2] However it was only in the thirteenth century that
it became definite. It then grew to be so generally accepted that

1. What follows is a development of my article, "A propos de la Lettre aux
Frères du Mont Dieu," *Collectanea O.C.R.,* 5, pp. 3–8, 81–95.

2. At least if one follows the Berlin Ms, Goerres 71, fol. 62ʳ, which origi-
nated at Himmerod, a foundation of Clairvaux in the diocese of Trèves. But
this is an isolated case which must be examined closely. All the other twelfth-
century mss are loyal to William. So are those of the early thirteenth century,
excepting those of the Pontigny tradition.

from the beginning of the fourteenth century William is not named in any manuscript.[3] This substitution is generally attributed to a copyist who was ignorant or at least not over-scrupulous. The ascription would then have been confirmed by a confusion between the appendix to the treatise, *On Loving God,* of St Bernard, sometimes called *Epistola ad fratres de Monte Dei de caritate,*[4] and the treatise with which we are concerned. The reasons for the interpolation certainly lie much deeper. The error of a mere scribe could not explain the existence of such a tenacious tradition. If there was a mistake, it was a deliberate mistake.

However it came about, this first substitution was the beginning of a remarkable history for the *Golden Epistle* and for William's teaching.

The book's introduction among St Bernard's works ensured for it a time of honor and tranquillity which was to last for four centuries. In 1662 there was a first awakening. Bernard Tissier, a conscientious editor of William's works, broke with the past, shelved tradition and restored the *Golden Epistle* to its real author.[5] Mabillon followed suit in his various editions[6] and everything

---

3. One then finds this strange state of affairs: fifteenth-century mss attribute the *Epistle* without qualification to the "divine Bernard," while giving, complete, the Preface in which William enumerates his works, with a generous supply of circumstantial details which ought to have aroused some thought. See, e.g., Bruges 115. Those who were responsible for the ascription, and their successors in the thirteenth and fourteenth centuries, had had enough daring and shame to make them suppress this compromising part of the Preface.

Two mss of the fifteenth century, preserved at Brussels, Bib. royale nos. 418 and 480-85, still bear William's name. But they are a faithful copy of a thirteenth-century ms, Brussels II—1064, which came from Sainte Marie d'Aulne, which gives a text of the *Golden Epistle* which is curious to say the least.

4. For instance, Bib. de l'Arsenal, Mss 500, fol. 107. On this subject see A. Wilmart, *Auteurs spirituels et textes dévots du Moyen âge latin,* Etudes d'histoire littéraire (Paris: Bloud et Gay, 1932), pp. 251-252.

5. *Bibliotheca cisterciensium,* 4:1-2: *In opera beati Guillelmi praefatio.* This preface has been reproduced in Migne: PL 180:202-206.

6. *Sti Bernardi abbatis primi Clarae-vallensis Opera omnia* (Paris, 1667, 1690) vol. 2, cols. 195-198: *Admonitio.* Reproduced in Migne: PL 184:297-300.

seemed to have been sorted out when, at the beginning of the eighteenth century, Martène, on the authority of a manuscript discovered at Pontigny, again snatched the *Epistle* from William of St Thierry, but this time in order to ascribe it to the Venerable Guigo of Castro, the fifth prior of the Grand Chartreuse.[7] In 1889, Gillet returned to the charge and took up on his own account the arguments of Mabillon and of the *Histoire littéraire de la France*.[8] Coming close to our own day Abbé Adam and the scholar Dom Wilmart have set themselves to dispose of the claims of Bernard and Guigo; the first in his fine thesis on William of St Thierry;[9] the second in a series of articles with plentiful documentation and a logic that can meet any test.[10] After eight centuries of uncertainty the matter is settled: the *Epistle to the Brothers of Mont Dieu* is really the work of William, St Bernard's great friend. So much for the "external" history.

There is another history, less eventful but just as strange: I mean the reception that the teaching in the *Epistle* had as time passed, an inner history in which can be found a golden age, a silver age and an iron age.

The first age lasts until the end of the fifteenth century. During this time the *Epistle's* prestige is very high. It is constantly quoted by spiritual masters to support their teaching and appears to be an eminently trustworthy document on which the Doctors of the Church did not hesitate to depend. St Bonaventure in the thirteenth century, Ruysbroeck and Tauler in the fourteenth, Denis the

7. Martène's arguments are found in the *Admonitio* of Massuet: PL 184: 299–308. Clément, in the *Histoire littéraire de la France* (Paris, 1759) 9:654ff, takes up Mabillon's thesis, while Ceillier, in his *Histoire générale des auteurs ecclésiastiques* (Paris: Vives, 1863) 14:308, defends Massuet's.

8. J. Gillet, *La Chartreuse du Mont-Dieu* (Rheims: Lepargneur, 1889) pp. 84–89.

9. A. Adam, *Guillaume de Saint-Thierry, sa vie et ses oeuvres* (Bourg, 1923) pp. 76–84.

10. A. Wilmart, "Les écrits spirituels des deux Guigues," *Revue d'ascétique et de mystique*, 5 (1924) pp. 59–79, 127–158; an article reproduced in *Auteurs spirituels*, pp. 248–259. See also, "La préface de la lettre aux Frères du Mont-Dieu," *Revue Bénédictine*, 36 (1924) pp. 229–247.

Carthusian in the fifteenth, to mention only the best known,[11] held the *Epistle's* teaching in high esteem; they drew inspiration from it themselves, and sent their disciples to it as to a spring of living water. In the midst of all this enthusiasm, Gerson's *caute legatur* carried little weight.

The sixteenth, seventeenth and eighteenth centuries are to some extent more reserved. The *Epistle* was still widely employed: Francis de Sales quoted it, Aloysius Gonzaga almost knew it by heart, Mabillon gave it the title of the *Golden Epistle* and finally Clément devotes to it some laudatory pages of his *Histoire littéraire de la France*. But these were mostly external tributes. The age of fruitfulness was over. Whereas the day before, the *Epistle* had seemed to be a small *summa* of mystical theology, it had become merely a manual of asceticism, a "directory" which was admired for its wisdom and discretion and which was often recommended. It was the silver age.

I shall say nothing of the iron age except that it is drawing to a close; after a period of oblivion when it was hardly mentioned except when the quality of its teaching was questioned, the *Epistle to the Brothers* has come out of the shadows and is now inspiring some interesting studies. We have even been led to foresee a new era of prosperity in which its author would appear as a personality of the highest rank.[12]

The intriguing thing about this second history is that it all hangs, so to speak, on the pen of an ordinary scribe. The greatness and fall of the *Epistle to the Brothers of Mont Dieu* seem to be inseparable from its ascription. The golden age and most of the silver age

---

11. We can add St Anthony of Padua, David of Augsburg, the Author of the Imitation, Bernard de Besse, Jean de Castel, Gerson, Hadewijch, etc. See J. Heerinckx, "Les sources de la théologie mystique de saint Antoine de Padove," *Revue d'ascétique et de mystique,* 13 (1932) pp. 225–256 and "Influence de l' *Epistola ad Fratres de Monte Dei* sur la composition de l'homme extérieur et intérieur de David d'Augsburg," *Etudes Franciscaines,* 45 (1933) pp. 330–347. See also J. van Mierlo, "Hadewijch en Wilhelm van Saint-Thierry," *Ons Geestelijk,* 3 (1929) pp. 44–59.

12. See Wilmart, "La préface. . . ."

exactly correspond to the Bernardine period. All the mystics mentioned above refer to St Bernard's authority: *Dicit Bernardus in Epistola ad fratres*.[13] This high patronage did give the little work an unquestioned authority and may be enough to explain its outstanding success. On the other hand it seems certain that when Tissier replaced St Bernard's name by William's, he struck a fatal blow at the reputation of the *Golden Epistle*. William was so little known, his writings had so small a circulation and his teaching was fundamentally so new! Before the little-known author of the *Mirror* and the *Enigma* had time to become known in his own right and anyone had recognized in the *Epistle to the Brothers of Mont Dieu* the sound and strong teaching of these enlightening treatises, a new name appeared on the scene. Almost as soon as he was put on the lamp stand, the lowly William had to give way to someone yet more lowly: the Venerable Guigo.

After Martène and Massuet, Migne's edition completed the work of confusing the issue: the *Epistle* is published among the works attributed to the holy Abbot of Clairvaux and is ascribed to the Prior of the Chartreuse, but at its head is Mabillon's note in favor of the Abbot of St Thierry: Guigo, William or St Bernard?

Today the story has come to an end. In the peaceful atmosphere which follows this sacristy argument which had its unedifying sides, we can at last study the *Epistle to the Brothers of Mont Dieu* and try to sound the depths of its teaching which was formerly so fruitful, knowing full well who is the author and in what context it must be read.

13. From Tauler (Sermon for the Nineteenth Sunday after Trinity) we have this: "An illustrious doctor of the highest rank says that at the very moment man turns to God with all his *mens*, with all his will . . . he recovers at once all that he had lost" through original sin. "Who is this *doctor insignis et excellens*, of whom Tauler speaks " asks P. Noël (*Oeuvres complètes de Jean Tauler* [Paris: Tralin, 1911] 4:194), "Perhaps St Thomas Aquinas?" No, it is William of St Thierry. For the *Epistle* reads: "Through sin nature has abandoned due order and departed from the uprightness with which it was created. If it turns back to God it quickly recovers, in proportion to the fear and the love which it has for God, all that it lost by turning away from him." (No. 88). This is one of the basic ideas of William's spiritual theology. However, the adjective *insignis* referred, in Tauler's mind, to St Bernard, not to William.

William or Bernard?

This former fruitfulness raises a difficulty and makes us ponder. We begin to wonder: Bernard or William? To which of the two does the *Golden Epistle* owe its success? History answers: Bernard. Certainly, but today we are arguing with history. The real author William does have something to be said for him. Would it not, strictly speaking, be right to pass on to him the praises which three great centuries lavished on this pseudo-Bernard? History seems to reply in the negative, pointing to William as the disciple and the interpreter of the holy Abbot of Clairvaux. The *Epistle* might be William's, but a William writing under St Bernard's inspiration and working over for himself the ascetic and mystical doctrine of the *Doctor Mellifluus*.

We cannot simply rely on the purely external evidence of history; we even have good reason to discount it from the start. Our predecessors trusted the *Epistle* because they thought it came from St Bernard. Now that the mistake has been corrected we must break with the past and ask if the *Epistle* has still the same claims on us when seen as one of William's works.

That is not all: the *Epistle* used to be understood in the light of the writings of the great monk of Clairvaux. But we cannot follow this path. We must study William in the light of William. His own works, which fortunately are not lacking, must be searched for the principles which were able to produce the spirituality of the *Epistle*. This productive writer certainly had a theology! We must pick it out so that we can present its elements in an ordered synthesis. Only then shall we be able to assess and rectify, if necessary, the evidence of history. We may even find for the Bernard who made the *Epistle's* early story so triumphant, an imitator, a companion, and a rival!

I say "a rival," meaning that an objective study, as envisaged above, may be able to provide us with a counterbalance to the golden age: William's personality may restore to the *Epistle* the prestige it lost along with Bernard's name.

Let it be clear: there is no question of involving William in an attack on his Master nor of setting the two in opposition to each other nor even of eliminating the question of their mutual influence. It is only a matter of drawing the author of the *Epistle* out of Bernard's shadow—not because the shadow oppresses but because it conceals William's originality.

The position of the former Abbot of St Thierry is not exceptional; the last Father of the Church spread his white cloak over a whole group of mystical writers, preserving them, if I may say so, from oblivion, and also from malevolent attacks. Perhaps they paid too high a price for this paternal protection. They slipped into the background—as befitted their modesty—but their teaching followed them; a loss, for although we can still hear the basic notes of Cistercian mysticism, the harmonies escape us. It is really from the combination that the whole derives its complete beauty. It is not an attempt to dispute what Dom le Bail calls St Bernard's "father-hood by inspiration"[14] if one tries to draw out from under his mantle an Aelred, an Adam or a Hélinand, and to discern what there is in their spirituality that is original, personal and even alien to the Doctor of Clairvaux. In my opinion it is more of a tribute to the greatness and fruitfulness of his spirit; it is to throw light on the spirit itself by showing to some extent its effect on other souls and its development in other hearts. Above all it is to draw into the light the adaptability and harmony of one of the richest schools of mysticism which history ever knew, the original Cistercian School.

As far as William is concerned, it is to do even more. For this son of St Benedict, who passed from black to white out of pure love for the Cistercian ideal, is an unrivaled witness to St Bernard's spirit. No one penetrated farther than he did into the heart and soul of his holy friend, and no one became a more humble or devoted follower of him. Along with these great privileges there is the fact that William had the merit of knowing how to preserve "alongside an unreserved admiration for the Abbot of Clairvaux a complete

14. "St Bernard," *Dictionnaire de Spiritualité*, 1:1493.

independence in thought."[15] To the very end he remained the
thinker, the theologian, the "reasoning mystic" of his earliest days
as abbot. And, as we shall see, it was on personal and deeply original
lines that he built this work, which is so reminiscent of the school of
Clairvaux, the *Epistle to the Brothers of Mont Dieu*.

William's Epistle

Bernard or William? . . . Since the question has been raised, let
us try to answer it or at least to cast a little light on it. For this
purpose we shall leave the shifting ground of history and turn our
attention simply to the text of the *Epistle*.

Let us first look at the plan, simple as it is, of the work.

After some introductory paragraphs, which are simultaneously a
description and an eulogy of the Carthusian life,[16] the author comes
to grips with his subject and presents to us the "three states" or
rather, the "three ages" of the religious life: the animal state which
is that of beginners, the rational state or that of those who make
progress and the spiritual state or that of the perfect.[17] Each of these
states is studied separately. In the *Epistle* William was writing
mainly for novices, so he dealt at some length with the animal state
which, he tells us, is mainly concerned with forming the outer man,
with controlling vices and with purifying the soul.[18] He sketches
for the younger brothers of Mont Dieu a plan of ascetic life which
is very enlightened and entirely Benedictine in its discretion.[19]
Then, coming to the details of monastic obligations, he gives
complete directions for the Divine Office, *lectio divina*, manual work,
food and sleep.[20] This is the most highly developed part, and is
certainly the one that has attracted most attention and has made
the *Golden Epistle* an "ascetic manual" in the strict sense.

15. E. Gilson, *The Mystical Theology of St Bernard* (New York: Sheed and
Ward, 1955), p. 198.

16. Nos. 1–40.　　　17. Nos. 41–45.　　　18. No. 45.
19. Nos. 46–109.　　20. Nos. 110–139.

Before broaching the subject of the second state, William allowed himself a few asides and touched on matters of local interest: that of admission to the solitary life[21] and that of the construction of cells which he found, during his stay at Mont Dieu, too luxurious and too little in keeping with the spirit of poverty appropriate to a way of life as holy as that of the Carthusians.[22] After a section dealing at a very lofty level with prayer,[23] William went on to write on the reasoning state and the spiritual state.[24] These two stages of religious life are only sketched in, but sketched in by a master's hand. The last two chapters of the *Epistle* are not the least solid or the least profound: they have incomparable riches to offer when pondered.[25]

Clearly nothing could be less like a dogmatic treatise than the *Epistle to the Brothers of Mont Dieu*. This manual of spirituality is a detailed directory of the religious life and a mirror of monastic *conversatio*. At first sight it seems to have no properly theological pretensions, but we shall see that this is a mere appearance which does not stand up to a careful reading.

But let it be clear that the *Epistle* itself has neither the form nor the tone of a "treatise." It presents itself mainly as the overflowing of a benign old monk who wishes to share his experience of God with other souls already filled with the Holy Spirit. Although it is addressed to novices, it appears to assume in its readers an advanced

21. Nos. 140–146.   22. Nos. 147–168.   23. Nos. 169–186.
24. Nos. 187–300.

25. The division of this work is problematic. Hortius, followed by Mabillon, divided it into sixteen chapters, seventy-one paragraphs. "The division adopted by Massuet, which is Migne's, is not a happy one."—A. Wilmart (*Auteurs spirituels,* p. 250, note 1). The oldest ms tradition is unanimous in dividing the little work into two books. This division is found in the fifteenth century mss along with the subdivision into chapters. The tone of the two books is, moreover, different enough to justify this division in William's thought. It is clear that the first is primarily addressed to novices. On the other hand, the questions raised in the second book presuppose a certain amount of spiritual maturity, a formed spirit, open to subtle points of philosophy and already initiated into the secrets of the mystical life. While respecting this division into books, I hope I have found a more satisfactory arrangement than that of Migne.

B

acquaintance with the mysterious realities with which it deals. It is rich in doctrine but does not claim to say everything; it aims at giving light rather than instructing, at encouraging and stimulating rather than building.

In short it has the simplicity and attraction of an intimate letter.

This is a first impression which is indeed very true and very characteristic, but which one is soon tempted to revoke. It is in fact impossible not to be struck, as one reads, by the attractive teaching of some chapters, and especially by the numerous discourses on philosophy and other subjects. As one tries to go deeper one realizes that the author touches on a great number of problems, both theological and mystical; but one thinks that his wish to be comprehensive has clashed with the need to be brief or with a desire to remain simple and accessible to everyone. In the last chapter, among others, there are several formulas which one suspects are very rich but which disappoint in spite of their liveliness and spontaneity. Here and there a shadow of vagueness flits over the text.

This is a second impression which certainly has some meaning but is not conclusive. A wise and well-meaning reader will take care not to yield to it. He will see the need to go still further and to dig still deeper.

Ascetical and Mystical

One thing seems to have struck and influenced the readers of the "age of silver" particularly: the obvious disproportion between the two main divisions of the *Epistle*, the development of the author's ascetic program at the expense of his mysticism. From the day when rigid barriers divided these two elements in the Christian life, a disproportion of this kind (whether or not it was intended by the author) could not help cast a shadow over one part of his work. The first part was wide open to everyone, the latter, the share of an elite! It was only one step from there to minimizing the importance of the author's theological teaching. It is not surprising, then, to see one critic of the *Epistle* quoting freely from the ascetic part but rejecting the mysticism as suspect and even dangerous.

Let us remember though that these censors did not know William and the fact that he wrote the *Epistle*. Therefore they could not understand the close bond between this small manuscript and the various works of the former Abbot of St Thierry. For want of the key to this spiritual castle, they remained on the threshold and did not suspect that the soul was inside! Is it surprising then that its mysticism entirely escaped them? But not only the mysticism! The asceticism too was not given its true proportions, was thrown off its course and misunderstood; the reversal of values led to meaninglessness and indeed to a radical deformation. It was not seen that for William, as indeed for all the writers of his period, asceticism only exists for the sake of the mysticism which controls and crowns it. Let us also note this fact: the *Golden Epistle,* the last of William of St Thierry's spiritual writings, is the only one which deals explicitly with asceticism. This in part explains the seeming lack of proportion.

However, the restricted form of the doctrinal and mystical part does not in any way entitle us to consider it negligible! Quite the opposite; these pages are a kind of reminder, an evocation or a schema of a far-reaching theology developed earlier. They deserve full attention and should be studied all the more deeply. If this element is eliminated there will no longer be anything more than a book of direction like so many others, a manual of asceticism, which is certainly very Benedictine in its discretion but with no originality and no life.

In the dedicatory Preface to his work William says: " . . . I decided that I should dedicate to you also . . . *The Mirror of Faith* . . . *The Enigma of Faith.* . . . There are besides other works of ours . . . . Read all these works then. . . ."[26] A pressing recommendation which is called for by the fact that the major problems touched on in paragraph sixteen of the second book of the *Epistle* are dealt with at length in the two treatises mentioned. (I would mention in partic- ular the delicate matter of the part played by the Holy Spirit in the

26. Nos. 4, 9, 14.

union of the soul with God.[27] It would be quite wrong to neglect William's advice for it is almost impossible to understand the spirit of the *Epistle* without having recourse to all these writings; they provide simultaneously the deep roots and the appropriate atmosphere. They are like dictionaries to which we must turn for exact meanings, the key to some of the formulas and the significance of some of the expressions. They are the key to the enclosed garden, the mirror in which William of St Thierry's thought is offered to us in its plenitude and purity.

What a remarkable work is the *Golden Epistle*, both in form and in substance! Here and there are new and bold ideas, daring formulas, standing out like medallions, which give such distinction to William's spirituality. Forceful reasoning, a gift for analysis, firm thought, keen speculation and a permanent alliance of reason and love prove him an ardent follower of Augustine. He asks of reason all that it can give him, but never tolerates any reason which does not end in some prayer and does not find its full development in some impulse of love.

The *Golden Epistle* reveals to us William of St Thierry, the "reasonable mystic" of the *Meditations*[28] and the treatise, *On Contemplating God*,[29] the "learned lover" of the treatise on love,[30] William at his most intimate and personal; and yet also the William of the *Mirror* and the *Enigma of Faith*.[31] Since he cannot embrace by

27. Nos. 263ff. See also, *The Mirror of Faith*, ed. Déchanet, pp. 162–164.

28. Ed., R. Thomas, *Oraisons Méditées*, Pain de Cîteaux 21–22 (Chambarand, 1964), trans. Sr Penelope in *The Works of William of St Thierry*, vol. 1, Cistercian Fathers Series 3.

29. Ed., J. Hourlier, *La Contemplation de Dieu*, Sources Chrétiennes 61 (Paris: Cerf, 1959), trans. Sr Penelope in *The Works of William of St Thierry*, vol. 1, Cistercian Fathers Series 3.

30. *The Nature and Dignity of Love*, ed. R. Thomas, *Nature et dignité de l'amour*, Pain de Cîteaux 24 (Chambarand, 1965), trans. J. Cummings, *The Works of William of St Thierry*, vol. 5, Cistercian Fathers Series 15.

31. *Mirror of Faith*, ed., J. M. Déchanet, *Le Mirroir de la Foi*, Bibliothèque de Spiritualité Médiévale (Bruges: Beyaert, 1946), trans. B. Babik in *The Works of William of St Thierry*, vol. 3, Cistercian Fathers Series 9; *Enigma of Faith*, ed. J. P. Migne (Paris, 1902) PL 180: 397–440, trans. J. Anderson in *The Works of William of St Thierry*, vol. 3.

intelligence alone the ineffable and inexpressible reality of God, he grasps him by love, a love which, for the soul confronting God, is a little like the blind man's delicate sense of touch, at least until the Holy Spirit "draws him into his way."[32]

All this constitutes overwhelming evidence in favor of William but seems to make the problem raised above insoluble. For if the impression of the Abbot of St Thierry on the *Epistle* is so striking and especially if the homogeneity of the *Epistle* and William's other writings is so great that it cannot be understood without them, how is it that our predecessors could have been so mistaken about it and considered as Bernardine a work that breathes William at every pore?

It seems to me that the answer is very simple.

Their point of view was principally "religious," monastic; ours is more "theological," I might almost say "scholastic."

From the religious point of view it is clear that the *Epistle* is entirely in the spirit of the holy Abbot of Clairvaux, with the same tonality as the *Sermons on the Song of Songs*.[33] The first chapters are strikingly reminiscent of one or other of those letters in which the great reformer takes on the role of fervent apostle of religious and monastic perfection. Elsewhere we hear a faithful echo of the *Apology*.[34] The *Epistle* reflects the monastic ideal in the twelfth century and embodies on the one hand the marvellous impetus which then seized religious souls and on the other it achieves a synthesis of the immense effort made by a monastic generation

32. For then, as we shall see below, there will be no more sensation, there will be understanding in a supra-rational way.

33. Ed., J. Leclercq *et al.*, *S. Bernardi Opera*, vols. 1–2 (Rome: Editiones Cistercienses, 1957–1958), trans. K. Walsh, *The Works of Bernard of Clairvaux*, vols. 2–3, Cistercian Fathers Series 4, 7.

34. For example in nos. 147ff, an appeal for poverty in monastic buildings (to be compared with Bernard's *Apologia*, no. 28, *Opera*, vol. 3, pp. 104–106, trans. M. Casey, *Cistercians and Cluniacs: St Bernard's Apologia to Abbot William, The Works of Bernard of Clairvaux*, vol. 1, Cistercian Fathers Series 1, pp. 63–66) and nos. 163ff, where William touches on the delicate subject of the monk's work. Throughout there is a deep affinity between the two works which was evident to monastic readers. In many collections the *Epistle* follows the *Apology*.

eager to pierce the veil of the divinity and to experience some of the secrets of mystical union. One might say that it is for the written tradition what the Abbot of Clairvaux is for the living tradition: a witness and exemplar of the Golden Age of western monasticism. We will recall the testimony of Denis the Carthusian on this point: "Whether it is by Bernard himself or—which is more likely—by one of his contemporaries, the *Epistle to the Brothers* is rightly ascribed to Bernard. For it could only have been written by someone favored by the same gifts of God, a kind of *alter ego*."[35]

Our conclusions from the theological point of view will be quite different; for on the ground of dogma it is not possible to bring the two writers very close together.

Etienne Gilson tells us that "William is distinguished from his holy friend by his greater fidelity to St Augustine."[36] He is distinguished from him even more clearly, in my opinion, by the impression the great Eastern writers have made on him and by his care to reconcile their teaching with his first Master's terminology. The few differences which I am going to mention here between William's theology and that of his friend, Bernard of Clairvaux, will indicate the very important problem which is raised by the inescapable fact of the Greek Father's dominating influence on William's thought.[37]

The Spiritual Doctrine of William and Bernard

William's spirituality, like St Bernard's, has the doctrine of the image and likeness running through the whole of it. But while St

35. "Verum, sive Bernardus, sive alius ei forsitan contemporaneus illam compegit *Epistolam,* ipsa vere Bernardo adscribitur, utputa eius personae aut alteri ei in gratia juxta quem modum amicus dicitur alter ego."—*De proeconio sive laude Ordinis Cartusiensis,* 5 in *Opera Minora,* 6:420B.

36. Gilson, *Mystical Theology,* p. 203. See also notes 24 (pp. 220–221) and 125 (pp. 236–237).

37. See my articles, "Aux sources de la doctrine de Guillaume de Saint-Thierry," *Collectanea O.C.R.,* 5 (1938–1939) pp. 187–198, 262–278 and "Autor d'une querelle fameuse, de l'Apologie à la Lettre d'Or," *Revue d'ascétique et de mystique,* 20 (1939) pp. 3–34.

Bernard places the divine image in free choice, William places it in memory, understanding and will or, to be more precise, in that higher part of the soul which the Trinity in creation marked with its own imprint and which should, according to the divine plan, be the seat of a constant remembrance, knowledge and love of God, in short of a higher, transcendent life, a real share in the life of God, three and one.[38]

The point that must be emphasized here is the nature of "shared life" which the concept of the divine image takes on for William. The image is not, as in St Bernard, a kind of divine jewel, which cannot be lost or destroyed and which is conferred on the soul like a title of nobility, granting it a likeness to God. Nor has it any more in common with the analogical resemblance which Augustine's psychology discovered and consecrated. It is "imprinted" in the literal meaning of the word, an indelible mark, the seal of the three divine persons, taking possession of the powers of the human soul from the moment of creation, so that before the Fall the soul found itself drawn, by its own natural structure, into the ineffable trinitarian movement.[39] This is what William calls creative grace.

The fall came to tarnish this image of the creator and to take memory, reason and will to some extent away from the divine possession. The living likeness has disappeared, but the elements remain and it is the grace of Christ or illuminating grace that now has the function of making present again in perfection, by and in the Holy Spirit, the original representation.

38. NDL, no. 3, ed. Thomas, pp. 22–26; Med, 12:14, ed. Thomas, pp. 94–98; NBS, PL 180:721B and 722B; below, nos. 209–212. In St Bernard's case I refer mainly to the treatise, *On Grace and Free Will*, c. 9, nos. 28–31, *Opera*, vol. 3, pp. 185–188, trans. D. O'Donovan in *The Works of Bernard of Clairvaux*, vol. 5, Cistercian Fathers Series 13. The great Doctor, however, is not unaware of the divine image as "memory–reason–will." See for example Sermon 155 of the *Occasional Sermons*, PL 183:665. It is not impossible to find in his works a conception of the imprinted image which is very close to William's, for example in the *Second Sermon for Christmas*, *Opera*, vol. 4, pp. 251–256; trans. R. Klienhans, *The Works of Bernard of Clairvaux*, vol. 4, Cistercian Fathers Series 10.

39. To be convinced of this one need only read attentively, giving due weight to all the expressions, no. 3 of the treatise NDL.

This doctrine of the image which is the nerve-center of the whole of the *Golden Epistle* is the ontological center of ancient anthropology. The Greek Fathers, as we know, carefully distinguished in man the body, soul and spirit or *voûs* in which was found the divine image. This trichotomy which is alien to St Bernard was taken over by William (*corpus—anima—animus*) and governs his whole idea of the fallen state and therefore his whole ascesis. For William, man before the fall is an "ordered microcosm": the flesh is subject to the soul, the soul to the spirit, and the spirit is itself naturally directed towards God. Sin is first and foremost a disturbance of this balance, a disruption of the movement of the soul drawn towards God. To re-establish the primitive order, to make the flesh "reasonable" and the soul "spiritual" and to restore to the spirit its original dynamism as a God-bearing creature, this is the aim of Christian asceticism, in William of St Thierry's view. Obedience, the first degree of humility, is the beginning of this path which leads to the heights of contemplation: at the summit is charismatic love, a perfect expression of the restored likeness.

St Bernard seems to follow the same road; he also starts from humility to end in love. But these are only two of the several nerve points at which for a moment the spiritual theologies of the two friends meet and intertwine.

The Theology of Love

Is there any ground that is more certainly common to the two Abbots than love? But nothing is less like love in St Bernard than is love in William! To convince oneself of this one need only read their respective treatises, *On Loving God*[40] and *On the Nature and Dignity of Love*.[41] While we find in St Bernard a description of love

40. *Opera*, vol. 3, pp. 119–154, trans. R. Walton in *The Works of Bernard of Clairvaux*, vol. 5, Cistercian Fathers Series 13.

41. Like the treatise, *On Contemplating God*, this work has been put under St Bernard's aegis. This explains why St Bonaventure did not suspect anything although he read the *Epistle* from a theologian's point of view.

that is essentially psychological: carnal love, mercenary love, filial love, wedded love; in his friend the dominant conception is of a more metaphysical kind. I will explain. For William of St Thierry there are only two loves: on the one hand is love "against nature," a sad consequence of the spirit's fall to which I have referred above. This is the love of unbridled concupiscence of which the Psalmist could say: "My heart (heart=spirit for the Fathers) has become as melted wax within me."[42] If it is not molded and raised, this degenerate love debases the soul below its proper state and leads it to ruin: καταβαθμός.[43]

On the other hand there is the love that is natural in the sense of being the love which corresponds to God's plan for man. This is the love of the heart that is upright and pure, of the spirit freed by grace, drawing the soul toward the heights. The steps of this love—was it William who first so conceived them?—are well known: *amor, dilectio, caritas, unitas spiritus.*[44] That is, as he more fully describes it in the *Golden Epistle:* inclination toward God, adherence to God, enjoyment of God, deifying union.[45]

Pure love as understood at Clairvaux is a kind of sublimation, an assumption of human love into the lofty spheres of the spiritual and the divine. Love as understood by William is, on the other hand, above all the communication on earth of the substantial charity of God: *"Amor noster Spiritus sanctus est."*[46]

There are very evident differences in the form of the two loves: the essentially affective one of Bernard, and the other, more intellec-

---

42. Ps 21:15 (Vulgate).

43. NBS, PL 180:725B; NDL, no. 2, ed. Thomas, pp. 16–18.

44. NBS, PL 180:724D.

45. Below, nos. 235 and 257. This gradation is not, as far as I know, found in St Augustine. St Thomas adopted it in his *Summa Theologiae,* I–II, q. 26, art. 3.

46. "Our love is the Holy Spirit."—*Commentary on the Epistle to the Romans,* PL 180:593C. See below, no. 170; Exp, no. 53, ed. Déchanet, p. 146, trans. CF 6:43; EF, PL 180:440A; MF, ed. Déchanet, p. 156.

tual, but without pride or rigidity, of the Abbot of St Thierry. The former evokes the ardent passion of the bride for her bridegroom, *fortis ut mors dilectio*; the other is more inclined to evoke a small child's reverent and tender love for its mother.[47]

There is no point up to the very end of the life of charity where we cannot find grounds for contrasting the two great friends. Certainly for both of them the end is, in the Spirit and by the Spirit, union with God and the knowledge which springs from this. But another difficulty arises as to the exact nature of this knowledge. I shall merely touch on this problem which is as delicate as it is important.

47. While the bridegroom loves the bride inasmuch as she is other than himself and because he wishes to be one with her, the child loves his mother "naturally," inasmuch as he has come from her, and is something of herself: her image. This is the *physical* love which P. Rousselot finds in St Thomas, Hugh of St Victor, and even St Bernard, and which he thinks can be opposed to *ecstatic* love which would be met, as an idea, in Richard of St Victor and especially in Abelard (P. Rousselot, *Pour l'histoire du problème de l'amour au Moyen-Age* [Paris:Vrin, 1933]. Is there really any formal opposition between these two conceptions, as P. Rousselot would have it? The first, the *physical* conception, is essentially theoretical and of the philosophical order; the other is rather of the practical order. St Thomas, for instance will give a definition of love according to the idea of beings: God-creature. In short it remains abstract. The others are more concrete and take more account of history, i.e., original righteousness-the fall-redeeming grace.

It is easy to realize that representatives of the *physical* conception, such as William of St Thierry, would gladly move into the group of *ecstatics* as soon as they stopped theorizing. In fact theoretically we love God because we came from him and are returning to him. Our love, says William, is "natural," *a Creatore inditus,* it is a "weight that draws us to the place of our birth."— NDL, no. 1, ed. Thomas, p. 10. But since the fall and because of sin, God has in a sense become strange to us (P. Rousselot's duality) and we love him first as other. But this "ecstatic" love nevertheless tends to put us back into the primitive order, to reestablish a state of things in which the interests of the lover and the loved one will again coincide. Also it takes us away from, no ourselves as P. Rousselot thinks, but that in us which has become evil through sin. It does not take us out of our deformed being, except to restore us to our "to be" as creatures in God's image. When this is done, this "ecstatic" love again becomes "physical and natural." At least this is what emerges clearly from the Prologue of NDL. P. Rousselot, who quotes part of it, could have found something better to support his thesis.

Love is Knowledge

Amor ipse notitia est: amor ipse intellectus est. Love (of God) is knowledge, love is understanding.[48] What does this mean? If we believe E. Gilson, that judicious interpreter of the Mellifluous Doctor:

> The soul *feels* God, when it loves God; it feels him by that very love it has for him and by the joy it finds in it; therefore it knows God. To this, it would seem, is to be reduced the famous doctrine of charity as vision of God. . . . Useless therefore to scan William's metaphorical expressions for a mysterious meaning they do not possess. No matter what image he uses, never does he mean to say that charity gives us that knowledge, sight or vision of God which here below is refused to every intelligence. . . . All that William would say is that in default of a knowledge which is and remains impossible, love, in us, replaces it; which is not to say that they are one.[49]

I hope Gilson will forgive me, but I must admit that I do not recognize William's living doctrine in this subtle dialectic. The impression that is left on me by this text and those that follow it is that the eminent professor, while interpreting William, is continuing to walk in St Bernard's path. I fear too that in this combination of charity and knowledge he exaggerates the part played by the Augustinian theory of sensation and cognition, which has already been advocated by L. Malevez.[50]

In my opinion, to understand this mysterious formula which is

48. According to P. Rousselot, this formula originally came from St Gregory the Great: "Dum enim audita supercoelestia amamus, amata jam novimus, quia *amor ipse notitia est.*"—*Homily Twenty-seven on the Gospel,* PL 76:1207. But the idea is earlier than St Gregory. It comes from the East.

49. Gilson, *Mystical Theology,* pp. 209–210.

50. L. Malevez, "La doctrine de l'Image et de la connaissance mystique chez Guillaume de Saint-Thierry," *Recherches de science religieuse,* 22 (1932) pp. 270–277.

the refrain of William's *Exposition on the Song of Songs*,[51] the *Mirror of Faith* must be turned towards it. It is particularly necessary to compare it with the "spiritual state" which is the crown of the *Golden Epistle* and in which William presents the soul to us as "informed" by the Holy Spirit and thereby penetrating to the depths of God. "Who then knows what is in man, if not the spirit of the man? and who knows what is in God, if not the spirit of God?" William goes on to say: "Men may teach how to seek God, and angels how to adore him, but he alone teaches how to find him, possess him and enjoy him."[52] This is the nerve center of the doctrine of *amor-intellectus*, rather than St Augustine's theory about the process of cognition.[53]

51. See the analytic index in volume two of *The Works of William of St Thierry*, CF 6:167.

52. Below, no. 266. The idea is developed at length in CG, no. 11, ed. Hourlier, pp. 102–106, trans. CF 3:53ff.

53. The part played by the Holy Spirit in "loving understanding" is usually passed over in silence by scholastic interpreters of William's thought. The rigid law of appropriation, no doubt. E. Gilson, who usually gets to close grips with the texts, makes no mention of it in treating of charity as knowledge, which must, however, have been very tempting (pp. 208–210). This is a serious gap which cannot be redeemed by the powerful reasoning. The remarkable interpreter of "sensation and cognition" keeps himself on a plane that is too exclusively natural and human. In various places William speaks of the *sense of love*. To understand this formula it is necessary to remember the divine origin of this love in William's scheme of things. Only in God is love at home: "Therefore its first place of birth is God. There it is born, there nourished, there brought up; there is its city, it is not a stranger but a native."— NDL, no. 3, ed. Thomas, p. 24. Communicated to the creature, perverted by sin, but restored and purified by grace, it preserves, in a regenerated man, the cognitive properties which it has in the Triune God. No doubt divine love is "powerless to grant us the knowledge, sight and vision of God which is denied in this world to the understanding." But it does better, since it gives us a knowledge of God which goes beyond this human understanding, a supra-rational, mystical knowledge, which, as such, is very difficult to define. This, I believe, is William's point of view, without doing any violence to the expressions. It is quite possible that a scholastic reader, accustomed to clear concepts, may be disconcerted by the shadows and imprecisions of this. But that does not confer any right to deny what William never tired of repeating (and certainly we cannot think he was playing with words): "No one," he says, "knows the Father except the Son, and no one knows the Son except

Let us note that, for our author, not all love for God is "knowledge"; but only the love described as "charismatic," the love of the *unitas spiritus*, the enlightened love of the *voûs* brought into unity by the Holy Spirit. Now for William the Holy Spirit is not only the reciprocal love of the Father and the Son within the Trinity: he is in all truth their mutual knowledge; he is not "love" but "charity," or, still following the author of the *Mirror of Faith*, "loving knowledge," "knowing love."[54]

This is why, once man's soul has been "spiritualized," it loves in knowing and knows in loving, not, certainly, in a human manner but *divino modo*, with a higher pneumatic knowledge, as the Fathers said. Understanding love is not the annihilation of the understanding but its assumption or sublimation; and it is the Holy Spirit, the enlightening knowledge of the hidden God, who makes this synthesis, if I may call it that, of the soul's two great faculties, "those two eyes of charity for divine contemplation."[55]

Amor ipse intellectus est. In the Holy Spirit, love is understanding. It is a real form of knowledge but one that goes beyond all human understanding; it is a direct and full taking possession, but on a superhuman level; and it would be minimizing William's formula to reduce charismatic love (I insist on this adjective) to a mere sensation or affective perception of God's presence.[56] That might be

---

the Father, and *him to whom they choose to reveal him.* These are our Lord's own words. They do reveal him then to some. . . . To those to whom they give generously the Holy Spirit who is their mutual knowledge."—MF, ed. Déchanet, pp. 162–164.

54. MF, *ibid.*

55. "Visus ad videndum Deum, naturale lumen animae . . . charitas est. Sunt autem duo oculi in hoc visu ad lumen quod Deus est videndum naturalis quadam intentione semper palpitantes, amor et ratio."—NDL, no. 21, ed. Thomas, p. 84. See also the enlightening text: "Duo sunt oculi in hoc contempla-tionis. . . ."—Exp, no. 92, ed. Hourlier, p. 212, trans. CF 6:74. These texts and other similar ones suppose the assimilation of love and cognition by seeing (vision-cognition) in William's thought. They contradict the irreducibility of love and knowledge generally accepted by Thomism. I shall return to this point.

56. If loving knowledge was only that, it would be hard to understand why William, dealing explicitly with knowledge of God, at the end of the *Golden*

St Bernard's point of view or that of a William interpreted in the light of St Augustine; but I am convinced that, in this matter as in others, William is a faithful heir of the monastic and patristic tradition of the East.[57]

Conclusion

The first point that stands out—or should stand out—is certainly that of William of St Thierry's strong personality and, as a corollary, that of the originality and complete independence of the teaching in the *Golden Epistle*. When it comes to judging and assessing a man historians sometimes write too quickly: ". . . this William of St Thierry whose name has survived less perhaps because of his writings and virtues than by his link with the Abbot of Clairvaux."[58] The university professor who wrote these words would, I think, be hard put to it to justify them.

Certainly William owed a great deal to his holy friend: his mystical vocation and the courage to carry it to fulfillment. It is

---

Epistle, twice returns to the leading part played by love in this knowledge: "But what he (God) is in himself, his essence, can only be grasped by thought at all insofar as the perception of enlightened love reaches out to it." (no. 292); "Yet humble and enlightened love attains to a more certain perception of it [God's life] than any effort of the reason to grasp it by thought. . . . " (no. 294). These are certainly something more than mere metaphors.

57. I was already convinced when I happened to have the chance to read the very original study of Madame Lot-Borodine, "La doctrine de la Déification dans l'Eglise grecque jusqu'au XIe siècle, "*Revue d'histoire des religions,* 105:5–43; 106:525–574; 107:8–55. It was a happy surprise for me to find in this enlightening synthesis most of the elements which, after several years of study of William, I had succeeded in collecting from his spirituality. E. Gilson recommends a study of these suggestive pages to anyone who wishes to grasp the background of the Cistercian concept of deification. As far as William is concerned, I have no hesitation in saying that Madame Lot-Borodine's study is very revealing. The θεωρία of the old masters, as it is presented to us, throws a very vivid light on William's doctrine and provides a key to many formulas.

58. M. Demimuid, *Pierre le Vénérable* (Paris: Tequi, 1896), p. 73.

very likely that without St Bernard's encouragement he would never have undertaken the composition of such works as the treatise, *On Contemplating God*, the *Exposition on the Song of Songs*, and indeed the *Epistle to the Brothers of Mont Dieu*, which is, briefly, his *Apology* for the monastic ideal in its original purity. Finally one may believe that the patronage of the Mellifluous Doctor served as a safe conduct for his friend's work, especially during the anti-mystical reactions of the fifteenth and sixteenth centuries.

But none of this detracts from the objective value of William's various works. The *Golden Epistle* will bring out, with its accompanying notes, the homogeneity of his writings and will bring into full view, alongside the psychologist and moralist, the thinker, the experienced mystic and finally the theologian, bold and energetic, as careful to respect tradition as to build a bridge between the thought of the Christian East and that of the West (as represented by St Augustine). This substantiates E. Gilson's saying with reference to the mutual influence of St Bernard and William: "William undoubtedly maintains a very distinct individuality of his own; his work counts, and if it had altogether perished that of Bernard would not suffice to replace it."[59] By way of compensation, the lofty historical and doctrinal bearing of the *Epistle to the Brothers of Mont Dieu* will throw light on its strange story and will justify the need, which so soon made itself felt, to enshrine it, like a precious pearl, in a choice reliquary: the works of St Bernard.

A second idea aroused by the foregoing reflections is that of the profound unity—in the midst of richness and variety—of the original School of Cîteaux. Unity from the religious point of view, variety from the properly theological point of view.

I have picked out some differences between the spiritual theologies of these two close friends. They are not small. There are others. Perhaps one would find some that are just as significant if one compared St Bernard with some of his other disciples: Aelred,[60]

59. Gilson, *Mystical Theology*, p. 6.

60. See, e.g., A. Hallier, *The Monastic Theology of Aelred of Rievaulx*, Cistercian Studies Series 2.

Hélinand or Isaac.[61] This may surprise us; it need not worry us.
These dissonances only strike us because arguments between
"schools" have perverted our spirits. I have no hesitation in saying
that the differences that I have pointed out, which are so important
from our point of view, were merely incidental in Bernard's or
William's eyes. At his friend's request, William corrects, William
censors, one might as well say, approves, the treatise, *On Grace and
Free Will,* in which St Bernard expounds his doctrine of the divine
image, a doctrine basically different from that of the Abbot of St
Thierry.[62] William in his turn communicates or dedicates to his
holy friend one or another of his works. In this exchange these two
spiritual men, in the midst of their differences, had no thought of
arguing. Beyond the words, the figures and the ideas, we must see
the living core of this School of Cîteaux, if we are to understand
how it could be "one" when the masters were so little alike.

The real characteristic of the religious movement of which
Clairvaux was the soul, was a search for God, systematically
pursued by men who were sure that they would arrive. This
sureness came from the Rule which they professed to follow to the
last iota. They knew that this Rule, this plan for the active life,[63]
would lead them to the charity of God, the threshold of a quite new
life: the βίος θεωρητικός, the contemplative life, the treasures of
which are wide open for the disciplined spirit. About this the Rule
has little to say.[64] Every time St Benedict touches on this life (at the

61. See, e.g., B. McGinn, *The Golden Chain: A Study in the Theological
Anthropology of Isaac of Stella,* Cistercian Studies Series 15, especially the
conclusion.

62. On this point see the Preface, addressed by Bernard to William, *Opera,*
vol. 3, p. 165.

63. "Active life" is taken here in the earlier sense of the word, meaning to
strive to eliminate vice and acquire virtue.

64. It is too often forgotten that according to St Benedict, the Rule is only
a handbook for beginners: *minimam inchoationis regulam* (RB 73:8) and it seems
to me that from this point of view it would be useful to see it in the framework
of the *Itinerarium mentis ad Deum* of the Greek Fathers. The active life, βίος
πρακτικός, and the contemplative life, βίος θεωρητικός, are juxtaposed
and coinhere throughout this itinerary. A comparison of the Fathers and the
ascesis of the Rule would, I believe, assist in an objective study of St Benedict's
thought in its original purity.

and of the Prologue and in the chapters on good works and humility[65]), he stops short as if he were afraid to interfere with the work of the Holy Spirit in his disciples. For it is the Spirit who is the real master and guide in this hidden "mystical" life. He is the only one who knows the hidden things of the sublime θεωρία, of the truly divine life which the Fathers called "theological," and he can reveal them to whom he chooses. Bernard and William are aware of this; this is why they have such thoroughgoing respect for each other's theology. They both have only one aim: to reach God, to find God. They go hand in hand all along the way of beginners, which is dealt with by the Rule. They part on the threshold of the way of the "spiritual"; but they both go on with a very sure step, each in his own way towards that *perfectionem conversationis,* the secrets of which are poured out, according to St Benedict himself, in the writings of the holy Fathers.[66] William draws from Gregory of Nyssa, from Origen and from Clement; Bernard from St Augustine. What does it matter, since both in the end *"recto cursu perveniunt ad creatorem suum."*[67]

J. M. Déchanet OSB

---

65. RB 4 and 7.   66. RB 73:4.   67. RB 73:4 (adapted).

C

EDITOR'S NOTE

The translation presented here is based on the edition of the *Epistola ad Fratres de Monte-Dei* published by Fr Robert Thomas OCSO in vols. 33–34 of the *Pain de Cîteaux* Series and carefully compared with the translation of Dom J. M. Déchanet which is based on the studies he has done in preparation for the publication of a critical text. Fr Thomas in his edition retains the paragraph numbers from the Migne edition (PL 184) and we have also (in Roman numerals) to facilitate reference. However we have also incorporated the section numbers (in arabic) introduced by Dom Déchanet since these will be retained in the critical edition and become standard for reference in the future. We should like to thank Fr Thomas and Dom Déchanet for the kindness they have shown us in the preparation of this work, as well as the translator, Fr Theodore Berkeley.

M. Basil Pennington, OCSO

THE GOLDEN EPISTLE

PREFATORY LETTER

TO HIS MASTERS AND BROTHERS,
Prior Haymon[1] and H.,
Brother William wishes
a Sabbath of Delights.[2]

I ADDRESS YOU WITH A FREEDOM SO BOLD
as to seem lacking, perhaps, in due restraint, dearest brothers
in Christ. Forgive me, because my heart is wide open. Do you
also, I beg, open wide your hearts to welcome us,[3] for I am wholly
yours in him with whose tender love I yearn for you.[4]

2. Ever since I left you I have been devoting my daily work,
such as it is, not to you who have no need of it but to Brother
Stephen and his companions, the younger brethren and the novices
freshly arrived among you whose teacher is God alone, in the hope
that when they receive these pages and read them they may perhaps

1. The manuscript has here only the letter H., but it is clear that the reference is to Haymon, second prior of Mont Dieu (1144–1150). However, we do
not know to whom the second H. refers.

2. Is 58:13. Gilbert of Swineshead in his *Sermons on the Song of Songs*, 11:5
(Cistercian Fathers Series 14), comments at length on the mystical signification
of this expression of Isaiah.

3. 2 Cor 6:11ff.

4. Phil 1:8.

find in them something that will serve to console their solitude[5] and spur them on in their holy resolution.

3. I offer what I can, my good will; and I ask you to give it back to me together with the fruit it yields. David pleased God by his dancing[6] not on account of the dance itself but because of his devotion. Likewise the woman who anointed our Lord's feet was praised by him not for the anointing but for the love she showed[7] and because she did what she could.[8] Therefore she found justification.

4. Then I decided that I should dedicate to you also another work which the needs of certain brethren, troubled by anxiety rather than threatened by danger, drove me to write for their consolation and to help their faith.[9] Their grief causes me great joy, except that I cannot bear to see them in sorrow.

5. For so great is not only their faith but also their love that they feel the greatest aversion for anything that seems to be contrary to faith, and if they suffer the least assault or disquiet in this regard, either from the spirit of blasphemy or from the prompting of the flesh,[10] they consider that the delicacy of their conscience has

5. A monk withdraws into solitude in order to live with God. Therefore in his solitude he is not alone: "The man who has gone within is never less alone than when he is alone." (see below, nn. 30 and 31, pp. 19f). It is a solitude which indeed does know consolation. William had asked this as a very special grace in his *Fourth Meditation:* "Give me, O Lord, the comfort of my wilderness—a solitary heart and frequent communion with you. As long as you are with me, O my God, I shall not be alone; but, if you leave me, woe unto him that is alone. . . ."—*The Works of William of St Thierry,* vol. 1 (Cistercian Fathers Series, No. 3), p. 115.

6. 2 Sam 6:14ff.

7. Lk 7:47.

8. Mk 14:8. This is a favorite text with William. He will use it again below in n. 16, p. 15. See also Med 5:10; 13:1; Exp 16.

9. See below notes 12 and 13. This work was not written at this time but only dedicated to the recipients.

10. In MF 10, William speaks of these "two pestiferous temptations, impurity and blasphemy." "The thorn of flesh" (or again "the breath of impurity") and the "breath of blasphemy," instigated by the devil are the primary adversaries to the kingdom of God in us. They attack the very

incurred no slight hurt, even if it be only by something heard or by some impression received. Then it is pitiful to see how they lament, as if their faith had suffered shipwreck.

6. The same happens to them, coming from the darkness of the world to the practices of a purer life, as happens to men who suddenly come into the light after being in the dark for a long time; just as these, because their eyes are weak, find the first glare of the light painful, although it enables them to see everything else, so they are blinded at the first light of faith and are unable to bear its unaccustomed rays until their very love of the light makes them used to it.[11]

7. That work is divided into two books, the first of which, because it is straightforward and easy, I entitled *The Mirror of Faith*:[12] the second, because it will be found to contain a summary of the grounds and the formulations of faith according to the words and the thought of the Catholic Fathers and is a little more obscure, *The Enigma of Faith*.[13] My purpose in such an undertaking was rather to avoid that idleness which is the soul's enemy[14] (since both old age and ill health prevent me from taking part in the common work, not that I have earned retirement but simply that I am lazy and useless) than to attempt the instruction of others. For indeed teaching is not seemly in a sinner's mouth[15] and becomes those only who confirm by their lives what they instill by their words.

8. The first of these books teaches the unlearned reader the way in which he is to direct his steps, the second puts him on his guard

---

foundation of our relationship with God, our faith. In the Garden of Eden our first parents succumbed to the assaults of this twofold temptation and since that first sin the devil has continued the same tactics seeking to destroy faith and separate men from God.

11. The "short preface" which is found in a number of the manuscripts and in the Migne edition ends here.

12. Cistercian Fathers Series 9.

13. *Ibid.* These titles are drawn from St Paul, 1 Cor 13:12: "We see. . . through a mirror in an enigma (*per speculum in aenigmate*)."

14. RB 48:1. Cf. Sir 33:29; Rule of St Basil, 192.

15. Sir 15:9.

against the perils of the way. For our Lord also observed this order when he told his disciples: "You know both where I am going and the way there."[16] Therefore the Prophet says: "The wealth of salvation is wisdom and knowledge." [17] Again in the psalm we say first: "Day unto day utters its word," and then "night unto night imparts knowledge."[18]

9. There are besides other works of ours: two treatises, the first *On Contemplating God*,[19] the second *On the Nature and Dignity of Love*;[20] a book *On the Sacrament of the Altar*;[21] some *Meditations*[22] not entirely useless for forming novices' minds to prayer; and an *Exposition on the Song of Songs*,[23] as far as the words: "When I had passed on a little beyond them I found him whom my soul loves."[24]

10. There is also *Against Peter Abelard*,[25] and it was this which prevented me from completing the preceding work, for I did not think I was justified in enjoying such delightful leisure within doors while outside he, with naked sword as they say, was ravaging the confines of our faith. As regard what I wrote against him, because I drew what I said from the fountains of the holy Fathers, as I did in my commentary *On the Epistle to the Romans*[26] and in the other works of which I shall speak below, in which I have said little or nothing at all of my own, it will be better, if you think fit, to suppress my name and leave them as anonymous works, rather than let the partridge seem to collect what it has not brought forth.[27]

11. For I extracted also from the works of St Ambrose whatever he has to say on the Song of Songs, no slight work and one deserving of esteem.[28] Likewise from Blessed Gregory's books, but at greater

---

16. Jn 14:4.   17. Is 33:6.

18. Ps 18:3. Psalm references are given according to the Vulgate enumeration as this is the one with which William was familiar.

19. Cistercian Fathers Series 3:36–64.

20. Cistercian Fathers Series 15.

21. Cistercian Fathers Series 42.

22. Cistercian Fathers Series 3:87–190.

23. Cistercian Fathers Series 6.

24. Song of Songs 3:4.   25. Cistercian Fathers Series 42.

26. PL 180:547–694.   27. Jer 17:11.   28. PL 15:1945–2060.

length than Bede has done.[29] For Bede, as you know, made his collection of extracts into the last book of his commentary on the Song.[30]

12. If you wish to transcribe the *Sentences on Faith*,[31] which I drew principally from the works of St Augustine (they are indeed strong meat and weighty with meaning), they are more akin to the book I mentioned above, entitled *The Enigma of Faith*.

13. There is also another work of ours *On the Nature of the Soul*,[32] written under the name of "John" and addressed to "Theophilus." To this, in order to treat to some extent of man in his entirety (for it seemed to be fitting) I prefaced *On the Nature of the Body*.[33] My sources for the latter were the books of those who concern themselves with healing the body, for the former, the books of those who are anxious to cure souls.

14. Read all these works then; and if you are not the first to do so, at all events be the last, if you will have it so. They might fall into the hands of those who, while they do nothing themselves, tear to pieces all that others produce. Then I too would not escape unharmed, I who am an old man and tottering, as we read of Isaac,[34] tottering, I mean, not as regards my feet but in mind. Finally I prefer that if my writings be found of no use they should be delivered to the avenging flames by my friends, acting not as judges but as counselors, rather than suffer the malicious assaults of detractors.

15. It is in a spirit of peace that God has called us,[35] and it is not only in the Lord's sight but in the sight of men also that we have to study our behavior[36] so that, if possible, for our part we may be at peace with all men.[37] The Apostle exhorts us earnestly to make this rule for ourselves, not to trip up or entangle a brother's conscience.[38]

29. PL 180:441-474.
30. St Bede the Venerable, *Liber septimus in Cant. Cant.*; PL 91:1223-1236.
31. This work of William's seems to have been completely lost.
32. Cistercian Fathers Series 24.
33. *Ibid.*   34. Gen 27:1.   35. 1 Cor 7:15.
36. 2 Cor 8:21.   37. Rom 12:18.   38. Rom 14:13.

16. Yet the man who reads these works in a brotherly spirit, even if he does not derive any consolation or edification from them, will find nothing to scandalize him or arouse his ire as if against an over-bold writer. And, to say nothing of edification, a friend will bear with my folly, if folly there be, in this too, and will not put an evil interpretation on my simplicity, especially for the reason of which I have spoken above, namely that, wholly ignorant as I am of what is going on outside and broken not only by age but also by sickness, I needed this work as a means of delivering myself from idleness, which, as Scripture tells us, gives rise to many evils.[39]

39. Sir 33:29. In Déchanet, *Lettre d'Or* (Paris: Desclée de Brouwer, 1956), this paragraph is n. 17; n. 16 being omitted in the numeration.

BOOK ONE

INTRODUCTION

AS THE BRETHREN OF MONT-DIEU introduce to
our Western darkness and French cold the light of the
East and that ancient fervor of Egypt for religious observance—the pattern of solitary life and the model of heavenly conduct—run to meet them, O my soul, and run with them in the joy
of the Holy Spirit[1] and with a smiling heart, welcome them
devoutly and with every attention a dedicated will can show.[2]

2. Surely it is right to feast in the Lord and rejoice[3] because the
fairest part of the Christian religion, which seemed to come into
close contact with heaven, has returned to life after having died, has
been found after being lost.[4]

3. Our ears had heard tell of it, but we did not believe, we read
in books of it and marvelled at the ancient glory of the solitary life
and at the great grace of God manifested in it; when suddenly we
found it in the clearings of a wood,[5] on God's mountain, on the
fertile mountain,[6] where the fair places of the desert now wax fat
on its richness and the hills are girt with exultation.[7]

4. For there through you it now offers itself to all men and in

1. I Thess 1:6.

2. Compare the enthusiasm which William expresses here with that he
expressed in connection with his first visit to Clairvaux: *Vita Prima Bernardi*,
Book One, XXXIV; trans. G. Webb and A. Walker, *St Bernard of Clairvaux*
(Westminster, Maryland: Newman Press, 1960), c. 14, pp. 59ff.

3. Lk 15:32.   4. Lk 15:24.   5. Ps 131:6.
6. Ps 67:16.   7. Ps 64:13.

you it displays itself. Hitherto unknown, it stands revealed in a few simple men. He who brings it among us is the same who by means of a few simple men subjected the whole world to himself, to the amazement of that world.

5. For although the miracles which our Lord wrought on earth were great and such as only God could work, yet this one surpassed all others in splendor and shed its light on all the others, the fact that, as has been said, by means of a few simple men, he brought beneath his yoke the whole world and all its lofty wisdom; and this miracle he has now begun to work in you.[8]

6. "Be it so, Father, since this finds favor in your sight.[9] You have hidden all this from the wise and the prudent of this world and revealed it to little children."[10] "Do not be afraid then, you, my little flock," says the Lord, "but show utter trust, because your Father has determined to give you his kingdom."[11]

II. 7. Consider, brethren, the circumstances of your own calling.[12] Where is the wise man among you? Where is the scribe? Where is the philosopher of this world? [13] Although there are among you some wise men it is by the means of simple men that he added the wise to your ranks, he who of old subjected the kings and the philosophers of this world to himself by means of fishermen.

8. By all means then allow the wise men of this world, puffed up as they are with its spirit, caught up in lofty thoughts while they lick the dust, allow them to go down with their wisdom into hell. But do you, while a pit is being dug for the sinner,[14] continue as you began: fools for God's sake,[15] through God's folly which is wiser than all men's,[16] following Christ's leadership, make your own the humble art of ascending to heaven.

9. For your simplicity is already stirring up many to emulate you.[17] Your making do with essentials and your rigorous poverty is already putting to shame the covetousness of many. Your

8. Phil 1:6.   9. Mt 11:26.   10. Mt 11:25.
11. Lk 12:32.   12. 1 Cor 1:26.   13. 1 Cor 1:120.
14. Ps 93:13.   15. 1 Cor 4:10.   16. 1 Cor 1:25.
17. 2 Cor 9:2.

retirement is already inspiring many with disgust for the things which are seen to cause disturbance. If then anything is meant by encouragement in Christ, by loving sympathy, by common fellowship in the Spirit, by feelings of tenderness and pity, fill up my cup of happiness,[18] and not only mine but that of all who love the Lord's name;[19] so that by your zeal and your earnest quest for God's glory, your own great reward and the joy of all good men, this holy novelty may come to enhance the variety of the garment, decorated with the gold of God's Wisdom, of the queen who stands at the Bridegroom's right hand.[20]

III. 10. I say "novelty" on account of the malicious tongues (may God hide you from their attacks in the shelter of his face[21]) of godless men who, unable to overcloud the manifest light of truth, carp at the mere name of novelty. They themselves are old, and with their minds set in old ways they do not know how to think new thoughts. They are old skins that will not hold new wine: they would burst if it were poured into them.[22]

11. But this novelty is no empty pursuit of newness.[23] It is

---

18. Phil 2:1f.　　　　　　19. Ps 118:132.

20. Ps 44:10. The Queen here, of course, is the Church. William may well have drawn the inspiration for his imagery here from his friend Bernard of Clairvaux who in the *Apologia* which he sent to William compared the Church not only to Joseph's many colored robe (Gen 37:3) but also to this garment of the Queen: "Concerning the Church it has been written: 'At your right hand stands the Queen in a golden robe, interlaced with variety.' This is why different people receive different gifts. One man is allotted one kind, one another, irrespective of whether he be a Cistercian or a Cluniac, a regular or one of the laity." See Bernard of Clairvaux, *Cistercians and Cluniacs: St Bernard's Apologia to Abbot William*, nn. 5f., in *The Works of Bernard of Clairvaux*, vol. 1, CF 1:38ff.

21. Ps 30:121. The "face of God" is a theme very dear to William and often occurring in his writings. See Exp 35 and note 17 there, CF 6:38.

22. Mt 9:17.

23. William must have been very conscious of the charge of "novelty" which had been levelled by so many of the traditional monks against his own order of Cîteaux. See, for example, Orderic Vital, *Hist. Eccles.* 3:8 (PL 188:637); Peter the Venerable, *ibid.*, 13:4 (PL 188:935); see also Jean Leclercq, "The Intentions of the Founders of the Cistercian Order" in *The Cistercian Spirit* (Cistercian Studies Series 3), p. 121.

something which belongs to religion from the earliest times, the perfection of that piety which is founded on Christ, an ancient heirloom of God's Church, prefigured from the time of the Prophets.[24] When the Sun of new grace rose it was already being restored and renewed by John the Baptist,[25] it was assiduously practiced by our Lord himself[26] and longed for by his disciples even while he was still present.

12. When those who were with him on the holy mount[27] had seen the glory of his Transfiguration, Peter at once was rapt out of himself and did not know what he was saying,[28] for the sight of our Lord's majesty inspired him with the wish to subordinate the common good to his own personal enjoyment.[29] Yet he was in full possession of his senses and well aware what he was saying, inasmuch as the taste of that sweetness made him judge that it was best for him to remain in that state always. So he expressed his desire for this life in the fellowship of our Lord and the citizens of heaven, whom he had seen with him, in the words: "Lord, it is good for us

24. The Prophets Elijah, Elisha and others, by their solitary life prefigured the life which would be enjoyed by the Christians in solitary company with Christ.

25. John the Baptist spent most of his life in solitude in the desert; Lk 1:80.

26. Christ even during his active life frequently withdrew into solitude; see Mt 14:33; Mk 1:35, 45; 6:46; 9:1; Lk 4:1, 42; 5:16; 9:18; Jn 6:15.

27. 2 Pet 1:18.   28. Lk 9:33.

29. Peter seems to have failed here in desiring to remain enjoying personal contemplation of the Lord rather than ascending with him from the mount to fulfill the ministries which were necessary for the salvation of men. This calls to mind William's treatise *On Contemplating God* (Cistercian Fathers Series 3), where he envisions himself going up to the mountain of the Lord to enjoy a soliloquy with God but only for a moment: "For we shall come back, and that unfortunately, all too soon. Love of the truth does indeed lead us far from you [material concerns personified in the ass—see context]; but for the brethren's sake, the truth of the love forbids us to abandon or reject you." (n. 1) William always lamented like his fellow Cistercian abbots, Bernard of Clairvaux and Aelred of Rievaulx, that the duties of the abbatial office impeded his contemplation. But all these abbots alike taught that the duties of their ministerial office must come before personal enjoyment of divine contemplation. See Aelred of Rievaulx, *When Jesus Was Twelve Years Old*, 31 and note 63 there (Cistercian Fathers Series 2:38).

to be here always. Let us make here three booths, one for you, one
for Moses and one for Elijah."[30] If this request of his had been
granted he would doubtless have made three other booths, one for
himself, one for James and one for John.

IV. 13. After our Lord's Passion, while the memory of the blood
he had shed for them was still fresh and warm in the hearts of the
faithful, the deserts were filled with men who had taken up this
solitary life, embraced poverty of spirit and rivalled one another in
spiritual exercises and the contemplation of God, seeking a leisure
that would yield rich fruit.[31] Among them we read of those Pauls,[32]
Macarii,[33] Antony,[34] Arsenius[35] and so many other leading figures
in the commonwealth of this holy way of life,[36] outstanding names
in the City of God, honored with triumphant titles of nobility that
were won by victories over the world and the Prince of this world
and over their own body, won by cultivating their souls and
worshipping their God.

14. Let them be silent then who judge the light while sunk in
darkness, and out of the abundance of their ill will accuse you of

30. Mt 17:4.

31. "A leisure that would yield rich fruit"—*pingue otium*—an expression
used by Seneca to designate contemplation: *Letters to Lucilius*, 73:10; trans.
R. M. Gummere, *The Letters of Seneca*, vol. 2, Loeb Classical Series (New
York: Putnam, 1920), p. 109.

32. William probably read of the different Pauls in St Jerome's *Vita Pauli*
(trans. W. H. Fremantle, *Life of Paul the First Hermit* in *Nicene and Post-Nicene
Fathers*, Second Series, vol. 6 [Grand Rapids: Eerdmans, 1953], pp. 299–303)
and Palladius' *Lausiac History* (trans. R. Meyer [Westminster, Maryland:
Newman, 1965], cc. 20, 22, pp. 70–76).

33. William would also have read of the different Macarii in Palladius'
Lausiac History: c. 15, Macarius the younger, *op. cit.*, p. 51; c. 17, Macarius
of Egypt, *op. cit.*, pp. 54ff.; c. 18, Macarius of Alexandria, *op. cit.*, pp. 58ff.

34. St Antony the Hermit (†355) was best known through the life of him
written by St Athanasius (trans. R. Meyer, *The Life of St Antony* [Westminster,
Maryland: Newman, 1950]).

35. Arsenius (†413) is also spoken of in Palladius' *Lausiac History*, 7, *op.
cit.*, pp. 25ff.

36. "Way of life"—*conversatio*—a classical word in monastic literature to
indicate the monastic way of life.

innovation; it is they themselves rather who are to be accused of vain attachment to outworn ways. But you will always have both those who praise you and those who calumniate you, as did our Lord too. Disregard those who praise you and love in them the good which they love in you. Pay no heed to those who calumniate you and pray for them. Then, forgetting what lies behind you and leaving on one side the traps laid for you on your path to right and to left, press on to what lies before you.[37] For if you stop to answer on every subject those who praise you or to argue each point with those who calumniate you, you will waste your time, and that is no slight loss for your holy undertaking. For to impose a delay on one who is hastening from earth to heaven may not prevent him from arriving but none the less it does him great wrong.

V.   15. Do not be careless then, do not linger on the way. A long journey remains for you to accomplish.[38] For you have undertaken the loftiest of professions. It surpasses the heavens, it is on a level with the angels, it resembles angelic purity. For you have vowed not only all holiness but the perfection of all holiness and the utmost limit of all consummation.[39] It is not for you to concern yourselves feebly with the ordinary commandments nor to give your attention only to what God lays down as of obligation; you must seek his desires, fulfill in yourselves what is God's will, the good thing, the desirable thing, the perfect thing.[40]

16. It is for others to serve God, it is for you to cling to him; it is for others to believe in God, know him, love him and revere him; it is for you to taste him, understand him, be acquainted with him, enjoy him.

This is no slight matter, no easy goal; but he who, in his love, makes you such promises is almighty and good. He will be faithful in fulfilling them and untiring in giving help. To those who in their

37. Phil 3 :13.

38. 1 Kings 19:7: The words of the angel to Elijah as he sent him on his way to the mountain to see God.

39. Ps 188:96.   40. Rom 12:2.

great love for him pledge themselves to great things and, believing and trusting in his grace, undertake what is beyond their own strength, he imparts both the will and the desire;[41] and he follows up the grace to will by bestowing also the power to achieve. Let the calumniator calumniate as he will: if a man faithfully does what is humanly possible for him to do, God himself in his mercy will give judgment for his poor one, will champion his cause,[42] because the man did what he could.[43]

VI. 17. Yet, brethren, let all exaltation be far from the opinion you have of yourselves, from your littleness and lowliness, from your mouths. For exalted thoughts[44] are death and it is easy for one who sees himself perched on high to grow dizzy and be in mortal danger. Give another name to your profession, inscribe your work with another title.

18. Think of yourselves rather as wild beasts shut up in cages, as animals that could not be tamed in any other way and by the usual means men employ, and so style yourselves. Consider them as being far above you in strength and admire their glory, those men who are mighty with both hands like Ehud, the Judge of Israel, who used his left hand as readily as his right.[45] As long as they are allowed, they love to stay inside and devote their leisure with all devotion to the contemplation of truth in charity; then when necessity summons or duty impels, they go out without a moment's hesitation to give themselves to the practice of charity in truth.[46]

---

41. For the distinction which William makes between "will" and "desire" see Exp 76: "But good will is already the beginning of love. And a passionate will, directed as if to an absent person, is desire; going to someone present, it is love; then what the lover loves is present to his understanding."— CF 6:64. William therefore sees three stages, only the first two of which he mentions here.

42. Ps 9:5.   43. Mk 14:8.   44. Rom 11:20.   45. Judg 3:15.

46. The balance between "the contemplation of truth in charity" and "the practice of charity in truth" was a life-long tension for William of St Thierry. He speaks of it in the opening paragraph of his earliest work, *On Contemplating God* (CG 1) and in his *Eleventh Meditation* (Med 11:13), a work of his maturer years, as well as in this his penultimate work.

D

19. Take care also, servant of God, lest you seem to condemn any of those whom you do not wish to imitate. I would have you act while you are still sick the way he did in the best of health who said: "Christ Jesus came to save sinners, of whom I am the first."[47] It was no hasty untruth that Paul so uttered but a heartfelt judgment. For the man who thoroughly examines and so understands himself judges no one's sin to be as great as his own, since he does not understand it as he does his own.

20. I would not then have you think that the common light of day shines nowhere but in your cell, that the skies are not clear except above you, that God's grace is at work only in your conscience. Does God belong to solitaries alone? Rather he belongs to all men.[48] For God takes pity on all men and does not hate any of those whom he made.[49] I would prefer you to think that the weather is fine everywhere except with you, and to think worse of yourself than of anyone else.

VII. 21. Rather, in fear and trembling work out your own salvation.[50] Do not wonder what others are like but, to the best of your ability, what they may become through your influence; not only those who are now alive but also those who will come after you and take you as their models in the pursuit of their vocation. For it is from you, from your example, from your authority that all the future of this holy Order in these parts will derive its character.

22. You will be called its Fathers and Founders by those who follow you and they will revere you and imitate you as such. Whatever you decide, whatever through your practice and observance has become a custom will have to be practiced and observed by your successors without any deviation, and no one will be allowed to introduce changes. They will have the same regard for you as we have for the unchangeable laws of supreme and eternal Truth; everyone should study them and be acquainted with them but no one may question them.

47. 1 Tim 1:15.   48. Rom 3:29.   49. Wis 11:25.   50. Phil 2:12.

23. Thanks be to God, you will incur no shame and those who come after you will suffer no harm if you persevere devoutly and courageously, and they faithfully imitate you in your present observance. If there should still be any need for change this too God will reveal to you.[51] For with all due reverence to the holiness of La Chartreuse—and the highest praises are due to it—many things are necessary in the bleak and unending cold of that Alpine district which might well be dispensed with in these regions by men who are satisfied with essentials and seek voluntary poverty.[52]

VIII 24. Understand what I say, for the Lord will give you understanding.[53] Meanwhile I rejoice in you[54] and although I am absent in body, yet, present in spirit[55] and seeing your good order,[56] your fervor of spirit, abundance of peace, grace of simplicity, strictness in following out your profession, the very sweetness of the Holy Spirit in your love for one another and the accomplished pattern of piety[57] in your way of life, I exult with all my being as I call Mont Dieu to mind. And I venerate the first-fruits of the Holy Spirit[58] and the pledge of a grace which promises the growth of religious life there.

51. Phil 3:15.
52. The reference is to the Grande Chartreuse near Grenoble, the first Carthusian Charterhouse, from which all the others sprung and from which the Order takes its name. It was founded by Bruno of Cologne in 1084. His fourth successor, Guigo, around 1127 codified their observances in a book of customs, *Consuetudines*. Undoubtedly the founders of Mont-Dieu brought these *Consuetudines* with them and it is to these that William would be referring here. It was actually not until 1163 at the time of the third general chapter that the different charterhouses were organically united to form an order. Thus at the time William is writing the individual houses had complete liberty to accept or reject various provisions of the *Consuetudines* of Guigo. William shows here a remarkable appreciation for what today we would call the principle of subsidiarity, an appreciation of the fact that the local community needs to adapt the common customs of a monastic federation or order to its own local needs—and not indeed to make life easier but to live it with greater intensity and austerity.

53. 2 Tim 2:7.   54. Rom 16:19.
55. 1 Cor 5:3.   56. Gal 2:5.
57. What piety means for William is defined below, n. 26.
58. Rom 8:23.

25. Indeed the very name of Mont Dieu affords grounds for fair hopes: namely that, as the Psalm says of the mountain of the Lord, there will come to dwell on it "the race of those who seek the Lord, seek the face of Jacob's God; the man with unstained hands and clean heart, one who has not received his soul in vain."[59] For that is your profession, to seek the God of Jacob, not as the ordinary run of men do, but to seek the very face of God which Jacob saw, he who said: "I have seen the Lord face to face and yet my life was not forfeit."[60]

26. To "seek the face of God" is to seek knowledge of him face to face, as Jacob saw him. It is of this knowledge the Apostle says: "Then I shall know as I am known; now we see a confused reflection in a mirror, but then we shall see face to face;[61] we shall see him as he is."[62] Always to seek God's face in this life by keeping the hands unstained and the heart clean is that piety which, as Job says, "is the worship of God."[63] The man who lacks it "has received his soul in vain," that is to say, lives to no purpose or does not live at all, since he does not live the life to live which he received his soul.[64]

IX. 27. This piety is the continual remembrance of God, an unceasing effort of the mind to know him, an unwearied concern of the affections to love him, so that, I will not say every day, but every hour finds the servant of God occupied in the labor of ascesis

---

59. Ps 23:4ff.   60. Gen 32:30.

61. St Paul: 1 Cor 13:12.

62. St John: 1 Jn 3:2. William has combined here the sayings of two apostles, giving them as if they were of one in a single quotation.

63. This is a favorite citation of William's which occurs frequently in his writings, e.g., Exp. 28, 39, 172; NDL 5, etc. which, however, is not found in either the Vulgate or Septuagint versions. Undoubtedly it was to be found in a particular Latin version which William was familiar with, probably a rendition of Job 28:28. Or he might be influenced by a passage in St Augustine. See below n. 278f and note 36 there.

64. We see here how William has drawn out of Ps 23 a complete but concise doctrine on the contemplative life. The end is to gain the mountain of God, to see God face to face. To attain that end one must be a true "seeker of God," which means in practice to carry out the exercises of asceticism, to do good works with purity of heart.

and the effort to make progress, or in the sweetness of experience and the joy of fruition.[65] This is the piety concerning which the Apostle exhorts his beloved disciple in the words: "Train yourself to grow up in piety; for training of the body avails but little, while piety is all-availing, since it promises well both for this life and for the next."[66]

28. The habit you wear promises not only the outward form of piety but its substance, in all things and before all things, and that is what your vocation demands. For, as the Apostle says again, there are some who exhibit the outward form of religion although they are strangers to its meaning.[67]

29. If anyone among you does not possess this in his heart, display it in his life, practice it in his cell, he is to be called not a solitary but a man who is alone, and his cell is not a cell for him but a prison in which he is immured. For truly to be alone is not to have God with one. Truly to be immured is not to be at liberty in God. Solitude and immurement are words that denote wretchedness, whereas the cell should never involve immurement imposed by necessity but rather be the dwelling-place of peace, an inner chamber with closed door,[68] a place not of concealment but of retreat.

X. 30. The man who has God with him is never less alone than when he is alone.[69] It is then he has undisturbed fruition of his joy,

---

65. For William "piety" can sometimes be taken in the ordinary sense of religion, piety, devotion. But frequently for him it has the meaning of contemplation, mystical union with God. In this case it signifies not so much a passing experience, a divine touch, but rather a state of the soul, one in which the soul experiences God or seeks to experience him, as is brought out in the definition given here by William. For a parallel to this, see Exp 178 where he comments on the same passage from St Paul which he will quote in the following sentence.

66. 1 Tim 4:7f.   67. 2 Tim 3:5.

68. Mt 6:6. This is an allusion to the words of our Lord: "When you pray withdraw into your chamber and close the door on yourself."

69. *Numquam minus solus est quam cum solus est.* A saying of Scipio Africanus recorded by Cato according to Cicero, *De Officiis* 3:1 and *De Republica* 1:17. It is quite probable that William had as his more immediate source St Ambrose: "I am never less alone than when I am alone."—Letter 49:1

it is then he is his own master and is free to enjoy God in himself and himself in God.[70] It is then that in the light of truth and the serenity of a clean heart a pure soul stands revealed to itself without effort, and the memory enlivened by God freely pours itself out in itself.[71] Then either the mind is enlightened and the will enjoys its good or human frailty freely weeps over its shortcomings.

31. Accordingly, as your vocation demands, dwelling in heaven rather than in cells,[72] you have shut out the world, whole and entire, from yourselves and shut up yourselves, whole and entire, with God. For the cell (*cella*) and heaven (*celum*) are akin to one another: the resemblance between the words *celum* and *cella* is borne out by the devotion they both involve. For both *celum* and *cella* appear to be derived from *celare,* to hide, and the same thing is hidden in cells as in heaven, the same occupation characterizes both the one and the other. What is this? Leisure devoted to God, the enjoyment of God.[73]

32. When this is practiced in cells according to rule, with devotion and fidelity, I make bold to say that God's holy angels

-----

(PL 16:1203); "He is not alone to whom God is present."—*Commentary on Psalm* 38:9 (PL 14:1093). William refers to this idea in other places in his writings, e.g.: *Life of St Bernard,* nn. 14, 34; Med 4:9.

70. Throughout this passage William brings out how the mystical experience of God gives one a more profound knowledge of himself. When the soul is favored with the graces of union a phenomenon of "de-materialization" takes place. One becomes much more spiritual, in coming to know God in a new way one also comes to know himself in a new way. Intuitively he more easily turns in on himself, his power of reflection is considerably sharpened.

71. Memory here is taken in the ontological and Augustinian sense of the word to designate that faculty which is the recipient of divine ideas and of God himself.

72. *In caelis potiusquam in cellis.* The medieval spelling (*celum* for *caelum*) and similar pronunciation made the relationship of the two words seem plausible. William derives both from the root of *celo* (I hide). This is correct in the case of the latter word, *cella,* but not in the case of the former.

73. *Vacare Deo, frui Deo*—two expressions of the activity of the contemplative life, the first a classical one, the second a favorite of William which frequently occurs in his writings.

regard cells as heaven and take the same delight in cells as they do in heaven. For when heavenly pursuits are continually practiced in the cell, heaven is brought into close proximity to the cell by the reality which underlies them both alike, by the loving devotion common to both, and by the similarity of the effects they produce. Neither does the spirit at prayer or even when it takes leave of the body find the way from its cell to heaven long or difficult now. For the ascent is often made from the cell into heaven, whereas scarcely ever is the descent made from the cell into hell, unless, as the Psalm says: "They go down alive"[74] in order not to go down when they die.

33. In this way indeed the inmates of cells often go down into hell. Just as by constant meditation they love to pass in review the joys of heaven in order to desire them the more ardently, so also the pains of hell, in order to dread them and flee from them. And this is what they pray may befall their enemies: that they may go down into hell alive. But it is scarcely ever that anyone goes down from his cell into hell when he dies, because scarcely ever does anyone who is not predestined to heaven persevere in a cell until death.

XI. 34. For the cell cherishes, nourishes and enfolds the son of grace, the fruit of its womb. It leads him to the fullness of perfection and makes him worthy to hold converse with God. But one who does not belong to it or is brought in under false pretences it quickly disclaims and casts out. That is why the Lord said to Moses: "Undo the shoes from your feet, for the place where you are standing is holy ground."[75] For a holy place or holy ground is quite unable to endure for long the carrion of dead affections or a man who is dead at heart.

74. Ps 54:16. This is taken by William not as an imprecation but rather as a prayer, asking that our enemies might, while still alive, reflect upon the terrors of hell and thus be converted. In his *Sixth Meditation* (n. 14) William speaks of himself sometimes going down into hell: "When, therefore, I am driven out of heaven, I am so weary of my life that I am ready sometimes to go down alive into hell—may I never descend there dead!"

75. Ex 3:5.

35. The cell is holy ground and a holy place in which the Lord and his servant often talk together as a man does with his friend;[76] in which the faithful soul frequently has intercourse with the Word of God, the bride is in the company of the Bridegroom, the heavenly is united to the earthly, the divine to the human. Indeed as a church is a place holy to God, so the cell is the sanctuary of God's servant.

36. For both in a church and in a cell the things of God are practiced, but more continually in the cell. In a church at certain times the sacraments of Christian religion are dispensed visibly and in figure, while in cells as in heaven the reality which underlies all the sacraments of our faith is constantly celebrated with as much truth, in the same order,[77] although not yet with the same untarnished magnificence or the same security that marks eternity.

37. Therefore, as has been said, the cell quickly expels as an abortion the man who does not belong to it, is not its true son: it vomits him forth like useless and harmful food. The workshop of piety cannot long suffer such a one to remain in its bosom. The foot of pride comes and the sinner's hand carries him off to another place; he is cast out and cannot find anywhere to settle,[78] he flees in misery, naked and trembling, like Cain from the face of the Lord,

---

76. Ex 33:11.

77. In MF 17 William distinguishes two types of sacraments of faith given to us by the Holy Spirit: "All these things are done by the one and same Spirit just as he wills, establishing the sacraments of faith. Some are corporal and visible signs of a sacred thing, as in baptism or again as in the sacrament of the body and blood of the Lord; others are only sacred realities, hidden from reason, but they can be investigated by the spiritual mind under the guidance of the Holy Spirit." It is this second type of sacraments, through which God reveals himself and communicates himself directly to man, which ought to be constantly celebrated within the cell of the monk. Cf. below, 117.

78. Ps 35:12f. St Bernard comments with some humor on this "foot of pride" in one of his letters: "Only the humble man can safely climb the mountain, because only the humble man has nothing to trip him up. The proud man may climb it, indeed, but he cannot stand for long . . . the proud man has only one foot to stand on: love of his own excellent spirit, and so he cannot stand for long, because he is like a man standing on only one foot. Who can stand long on that foot, the foot on which they stood who did wickedness and fell: the angel in heaven, the man in paradise?"—Epistle 393:3; LBJ 217, p. 296.

the prey of vices and of demons, so that the first to meet him inflicts the death of the soul on him.[79] Or if he does continue in the cell for some time it is not through the constancy which virtue breeds but through an obstinacy that makes him wretched, and so his cell is like a prison for him or like a sepulchre that has swallowed up a living man.

38. However, the wise man will be all the wiser for the punishment of the fool,[80] and the just man will wash his hands in the blood of the sinner.[81] Therefore, as the Prophet says: "If you are converted, Israel, be converted,"[82] that is to say, attain to the summit of perfect conversion.[83] For no one is allowed to remain long in the same condition.[84] The servant of God must always either make progress or go back; either he struggles upwards or he is driven down into the depths.[85]

39. But from all of you perfection is demanded, although not the same kind from each. If you are beginning begin perfectly; if you are already making progress be perfect also in your doing of that; if you have already achieved some measure of perfection measure yourselves by yourselves and say with the Apostle: "Not that I have already won the prize, already reached fulfillment. I

79. Gen 4:14ff.

80. Prov 19:25. William seems to have adapted the text here to suit his purposes. At least the text as we find it in the Vulgate has the fool rather than the wiseman profiting by the punishment.

81. Ps 57:11. What William seems to be trying to say here is that the just man rather than be scandalized and weakened in his vocation by the defections of others will rather be drawn by the example of their weakness to see his own sinfullness and strive to purify himself through contrition and greater efforts toward the good.

82. Jer 4:1.

83. Conversion in the biblical sense is a returning toward God. In monastic vocabulary conversion signifies leaving the world and entering the monastery. But this process of conversion—dying to the world and living to God—continues throughout the whole life of the monk.

84. Job 14:2.

85. This argument is developed more fully and most beautifully in the well known passage of St Bernard's letter to Abbot Warren of Alps: Epistle 254:5, LBJ 329, pp. 410f.

only press on, in the hope of winning the mastery, as Christ Jesus has won the mastery over me. This at least I do: forgetting what I have left behind, intent on what lies before me, I press on with the goal in view, eager for the prize, God's heavenly summons in Christ Jesus."

40. Then he adds: "All of us who are perfect must be of this mind."[86] Clearly the Apostle's teaching in this passage is that the perfection of the just man in this life consists in wholly forgetting what lies behind him and pressing on with might and main to what lies before. And the place where the perfection of this perfection will be achieved is where the prize of God's heavenly summons will be grasped with full security.

86. Phil 3:12ff.

THE ANIMAL MAN

THE BEGINNINGS OF THE SPIRITUAL LIFE

A S ONE STAR DIFFERS FROM ANOTHER in brightness[1] so cell differs from cell in its way of life: there are beginners, those who are making progress and the perfect. The state of beginners may be called "animal,"[2] the state of those who are making progress "rational" and the state of the perfect "spiritual." Those who are still animal may on occasion claim forbearance in some respects in which no indulgence should be shown to those who are considered as already rational. Again certain things are tolerated in the rational which are not tolerated in the spiritual: everything in them must be perfect, calling for imitation and praise rather than for blame.

42. Every religious institute is made up of these three kinds of men. As each is marked by a name proper to it, so each is recognized by distinctive pursuits. All those who are born of the light[3] should

1. 1 Cor 15:41.

2. Animal is employed here in the sense in which it is used in the Vulgate text—*animalis homo*—to translate St Paul's *psychicos* (1 Cor 2:14). The threefold division which William introduces here actually has its root in St Paul. Although Paul more frequently contrasts simply the spiritual and the carnal (e.g. Rom 7:14; 15:27; 1 Cor 3:1; 9:11), he introduces in 1 Thess 5:23 the threefold: spirit, soul, body (*pneuma, psyche, soma*—*spiritus, anima, corpus*). This is taken up by Origen and transmitted to the tradition where it had a great influence on the Cistercian Fathers. See J. M. Déchanet, Introduction, Exp, pp. xiviii ff.; also M. Basil Pennington, "Three Stages of Spiritual Growth according to St Bernard" in *Studia Monastica*, 11 (1969), pp. 315ff.

3. 1 Thess 5:5.

consider carefully in the light of the present day what is lacking
to them,[4] whence they have come, how far they have come,
the progress of the day and of the hour.

43. There are the animal, who of themselves are not governed by
reason nor led by affection, yet stimulated by authority or inspired
by teaching or animated by good example they acquiesce in the
good where they find it and like blind men, led by the hand, they
follow, that is, imitate others. Then there are the rational, whom
the judgment of their reason and the discernment that comes of
natural learning endow with knowledge of the good and the desire
for it, but as yet they are without love. There are also the perfect,
who are led by the spirit and are more abundantly enlightened by
the Holy Spirit;[5] because they relish the good which draws them
on they are called wise.[6] They are also called spiritual because the
Holy Spirit dwells in them as of old he dwelt in Gideon.[7]

44. The first state is concerned with the body, the second with
the soul, the third finds rest only in God. Each of them makes

---

4. Ps 38:5.

5. Above William noted that the "rational man" was the man who was
guided by reason. Now proceeding to the next step he speaks of those who are
guided by the Spirit. As with St Paul, from whom he ultimately draws his
inspiration, he considers here at one and the same time the Holy Spirit and
the spirit of man. Under the impulse of the Holy Spirit the spirit of man
becomes spiritual, *pneumatic.*

6. *Quoniam sapit . . . sapientes vocantur*—"because they relish . . . they are
called wise." The translation loses an important relationship that is brought
out only in the Latin text.

7. Judg 6:34. The Latin text here is somewhat more complicated. To give
it literally: "Because indeed the Holy Spirit puts them on just as of old he put
on Gideon, as the clothes of the Holy Spirit they are called spiritual."
Déchanet has a good commentary on this: "However the Spirit of the Lord
puts on Gideon, Judg 4:34. The obvious sense of this text is that Gideon was
clothed with the Holy Spirit (as the Christian of St Paul is clothed with
Christ, Gal 3:27). However, William understood it otherwise, as is made
evident by the expression: 'Clothes of the Holy Spirit.' Thus we see what he
wishes to say: 'Filled with the Holy Spirit' the perfect are, in a certain way,
the clothes of this Spirit who dwells within them ('he puts them on')"—
Lettre d'Or aux Frères du Mont-Dieu (Paris: Desclée de Brouwer, 1956), p. 164,
n. 68.

progress after its own fashion and each of them has a certain measure of perfection proper to itself.

45. The beginning of good in the animal way of life is perfect obedience; progress for it is to gain control of the body and bring it into subjection, perfection for it is when the habitual exercise of virtue has become a pleasure. The beginning of the rational state is to understand what is set before it by the teaching of the faith; progress is a life lived in accordance with that teaching;[8] perfection is when the judgment of the reason passes into a spiritual affection. The perfection of the rational state is the beginning of the spiritual state; progress in it is to look upon God's glory with face uncovered;[9] its perfection is to be transformed into the same likeness, borrowing glory from that glory, enabled by the Spirit of the Lord.[10]

XIII. 46. To treat in the first place of the first state, animality is a form of life which is dominated by the bodily senses, that is to say, the soul is as it were drawn out of itself by the bodily senses, engrossed in the pleasure afforded it by the material things it loves, and thus it feeds or nourishes its sensuality.[11] When it enters into itself again and finds itself unable to take with it into its spiritual nature the bodies to which it has become attached by the strong glue of love and habit, it fashions for itself representations of them and with these holds friendly converse there.

47. Since it is accustomed to them and thinks that nothing exists except what it has left outside or brought back into itself, it finds its happiness as long as possible in living with bodily pleasures.

8. Prov 23:1f. As it is found in the Itala version which is quoted by Augustine in his *Commentary on St John*, tr. 84:1 (PL 35:1846f.).

9. 2 Cor 3:18.

10. *Ibid*. For a study of Guerric of Igny's parallel use of this same text, see J. Morsen and H. Castello, Introduction, in *The Liturgical Sermons of Guerric of Igny* I (Cistercian Fathers Series 8), pp. lvii—lxi.

11. The animal man is still under the penalty of original sin. The soul is captive of the appetites of the body and must overcome especially two evil inclinations, pride and concupiscence. As disobedience was the fall of Adam, so obedience is the first principle of the renewal of man.

When it is separated from them it can think only by imagining bodies. When it raises itself to think of spiritual things or the things of God it cannot conceive of them in any other way than as bodies or bodily things.[12]

48. This state turned away from God becomes folly when it is excessively turned back upon itself and so wild that it will not or can not be governed. But when it is torn out of itself by over-weening pride it becomes carnal prudence and seems to itself to be wisdom, although it is folly. As the Apostle says: "They who claimed to be so wise were made fools."[13]

49. However, turned to God this animal state becomes holy simplicity, that is, the will always the same in its attachment to the same object, as was the case with Job: "a simple, upright and god-fearing man."[14] For properly speaking simplicity is a will that is wholly turned toward God, seeking one thing from the Lord with all earnestness,[15] without any desire to disperse its energies in the world. Or again simplicity is true humility in conversion,[16] more concerned with the inner reality of virtue than with a reputation for it. The simple man does not mind seeming to be foolish in the eyes of the world that he may be wise in the sight of God.[17] Or again simplicity is the will alone fixed on God, not yet formed by reason so as to be love (for that is what a formed will is), not yet enlightened so as to be charity, that is, the delight of love.[18]

---

12. "The animal man," said St Paul, "does not perceive the things of the spirit of God." (1 Cor 2:14). As Dom Déchanet points out in his note at this place, this is one of the consequences of original sin. Created in the image of God, man is no longer in contact with his own spirit, with the higher part of his being, with higher realities, but, on the contrary, with his lower faculties he is almost entirely imprisoned in the realm of the sensible worldly. Here essentially is what is meant by the animal state of man. And it belongs to man with the help of grace to rise above the sensible and terrestrial, once again to become truly rational and with his spirit direct himself to God and to the higher realities with the help of the light and grace of the Holy Spirit.

13. St Paul: Rom 1:22.   14. Job 1:1.   15. Ps 26:4.

16. See above, n. 38, note 83.   17. 1 Cor 3:18.

18. William again traces out a threefold progression: the simple willing, willing informed by a reason, and willing that has been illuminated. A parallel consideration of this in relation to prayer can be found in Exp 17ff., CF 6:14ff.

XIV. 50. Simplicity then possesses in itself some beginning of God's creation,[19] that is, a simple and good will, the shapeless material, as it were, of what will be a good man, and at the outset of its conversion it offers this to its maker to be formed. For since together with good will it already has a beginning of wisdom, that is the fear of the Lord,[20] from it it learns that it cannot be formed by itself and that nothing is so advantageous for a fool as to serve a wise man.[21]

51. Accordingly it submits to a man for God's sake, entrusting to him its good will to be formed in God, in the feelings and the spirit of humility. Already the fear of God is beginning to develop all the plenitude of the virtues: justice, because it defers to a superior; prudence, because it does not trust in itself; temperance, because it refrains from deciding for itself; fortitude, because it submits itself wholly to obedience, concerned not to judge but only to do what it is bidden.

52. For this is the wife to whom the Lord said: "You shall be turned toward your husband."[22] Its husband is either its own

19. Jas 1:18. William's thought here is that at the moment of conversion the will turns itself toward God, the only step that is within its power to take. But this simple beginning opens the way for God to act, and that with ever increasing power and might. In other words, by his good will man presents himself to God as something on which God can work, which he can inform. We have here the idea of the will of man being formless matter which is to be informed or given form by grace.

20. Ps 110:10; Sir 1:14.

21. Prov 11:29. We can see here that William has studied at Benedict's "School of the Lord's Service," where it is taught: "The first step of humility is obedience without delay"—RB 5:1. William goes on, however, to demonstrate the traditional teaching of the inter-relation of all the virtues by demonstrating how obedience includes the exercise of the four cardinal virtues: justice, prudence, temperance and fortitude.

22. Gen 3:16 (Septuagint). In William's teaching here concerning the improper order of submission we can see perhaps the influence of John Scotus Eriugena who comments on this passage in Genesis: "In this place in Genesis the divine voice promises us the restitution of the natural order of human nature, the return to our original condition (before the sin of Adam). The order of nature is this: the spirit, submitted in complete obedience to the power of the Creator, adheres to God totally. And thus it follows that reason submits freely to the dominative power of the spirit. And then finally the

reason or spirit or that of another. This is the husband a simple
and upright man rightly obeys in himself—but often more rightly
and more safely in another than in himself.

53. The Lord's commandment and the very order of nature bids
a wife to make this rightful turning, that is, perfect obedience
toward her husband, and likewise they command animality to
turn in the same way toward its spirit or toward some spiritual
man. This perfect obedience especially in a beginner does not
include discretion, that is, it does not question what is bidden, or
why,[23] but all its effort is directed to the faithful and humble
accomplishment of what its superior commands it to do.

54. For the tree which gives knowledge of good and evil in
paradise[24] is in religious life the power to decide, and it is entrusted
to the spiritual father who judges all things while he himself is
judged by no one.[25] It is for him to decide, for others to obey.
To his undoing, Adam tasted of the forbidden tree, led astray by
him who made the suggestion: "Why has God commanded you
not to eat of the tree?"[26] There you have one questioning why the
command was given. Then he went on: "For he knew that on the
day you ate your eyes would be opened and you would be like
gods."[27] There you have what is commanded, namely that he
would not allow them to become gods. He decided, he ate, and,
falling into disobedience, he was expelled from paradise.[28] So it is
impossible for one who, in the animal state, decides for himself, a
"prudent" novice, a "wise" beginner, to stay in his cell for long or
to persevere in the community. Let him become foolish if he is to be
wise[29] and let this be the whole of his discretion, to be entirely

---

body remains under the yoke of sound reason. And this natural order assures
to the creature a harmonious peace with himself and with God."—*De
Divisione Naturae,* 4:25 (PL 122:855). For a study of the influence of Eriugena
on William of St Thierry, see J. Hourlier's Introduction to the treatise, *On
Contemplating God* in *The Works of William of St Thierry,* vol. 1 (Cistercian
Fathers Series 3), pp. 29f.

23. Cf. NDL 7.	24. Gen 2:9.	25. 1 Cor 2:13.
26. Gen 3:1.	27. Gen 3:5.	28. Gen 3:6, 24.
29. 1 Cor 3:18.		

without discretion in this.[30] Let this be the whole of his wisdom, to
be wholly lacking in wisdom in this respect.

XV. 55. However on the borders of animality and reason the
kind Creator has left, in the nature of the human soul, intelligence
and inventiveness, and in inventiveness skill.[31] So it is that God
established man over the work of his hands and put all the things of
this world under his feet.[32] To one in the animal state who is proud
this comes as a reminder of his natural dignity and of the lost
likeness to God, but to one who is simple and humble it serves as a
help to recover and keep that likeness.

56. So it is that what can be known of God is clear to them
within themselves.[33] And so it is that creation affords some idea of
the Creator.[34] So it is that God's justice is known[35] and also the
truth that those who do good are worthy of life, while those who
act otherwise are worthy of death.[36]

57. So it is that creation, of its own accord serving man, subjects
and adapts itself to his nature,[37] with the result that it serves that

30. As William expressed it in NDL (n. 7): "All his discretion must be that
he be a fool for Christ, and depend on the will of another."

31. William here, of course, is speaking of fallen man. God in his goodness
has left to him as a plank of salvation the use of his reason. But it tends to be
distracted and lost, as it were, as it is immersed in a world of sensible things.
However, rightly used the intelligence can enable him to so use the sensible
that he can through them come to his Creator. Along with intelligence man
has also inventiveness, genius, talent, which enable him to use the material
world intelligently. Along with this God has also left with man "art," the
ability of execution. To exemplify this (William will give other examples
later on) the intelligence conceives of the utility of building a house; the
inventiveness creates a plan; and art carries out the practical execution of it.
Or again, the intellect can conceive of a literary work and decide to do it;
inventiveness will determine on precisely how it will be composed, the order
of the composition; and it will remain for literary art to carry it out with
greater or less success.

32. Ps 8:7f.   33. Rom 1:19.   34. Rom 1:20; Wis 13:5ff.
35. Rom 1:17.   36. Rom 1:32.

37. We have here an idea which recurs in the writings of William and is
probably drawn from St Gregory of Nyssa, namely that man is the king of
creation and that it is placed entirely at his service. For a study of the influence

E

necessity which springs from sin, and it is at the mercy of man's will and pleasure.[38]

58. It is clear for all to see how many things and things of great importance which are needed for this life, which are of use both to the good and to the bad, which are very beautiful in their own order, have been made and are being made both by good men and by evil men using these same faculties.

59. Hence derive in the realms of literature, art and architecture, through the countless discoveries of all sorts which men have made, so many branches of learning, so many kinds of professions, precisions in scientific research, arts of eloquence, varieties of positions and posts and innumerable investigations into the nature of this world.[39]

All men avail themselves of these things for their needs and for their advantage, both those who are called wise in this world and those simple men who are God's sons.[40] But the former misuse them to satisfy their curiosity, their pleasure and their pride, while the latter render service with them as necessity demands, finding their joy elsewhere.

60. Therefore the former, enslaved to their senses and their bodies, reap the fruits of their flesh, which are fornication, uncleanness, impurity, feuds, quarrels, jealousies, outbursts of anger, factions, dissensions, rivalries, debauchery, drunkenness and suchlike which make it impossible for those who live in such a way to inherit God's kingdom.[41] Whereas the latter reap the fruits of the spirit, which are charity, joy, peace, patience, kindness, forbearance, generosity, gentleness, faith, temperateness, chastity,

---

of Gregory of Nssya on William of St Thierry, see J. M. Déchanet, "Guillaume et Saint Grégoire de Nysse" in *Collectanea O.C.R.,* 5 (1938) pp. 187–198, 262–278.

38. Even in man's fallen state creation still remains largely subject to him, but now he more commonly uses it to obtain ends contrary to the right order of nature.

39. 1 Cor 1:20.   40. Phil 2:15.   41. Gal 5:19ff.

continence[42] and the piety which promises well both for this life and for the next.[43]

XVI. 61. Both of them engage in action side by side and to men's eyes their deeds are alike but God sees how different are their wills and intentions. When each of them returns to himself his conscience regales him with the fruits of his intentions. Not, however, that both return to their conscience in the same way, since no one likes to return to it after action who did not go forth from it to act with a right intention.

62. However, a man who has not yet mastered his inordinate desires may recollect himself. Then he finds in himself the effects of those desires: either pleasures which charm him or wounds that are sore, and these give rise to many thoughts.[44] Another man may have mastered his inordinate desires without yielding his mind to the stronger attraction or the greater pleasure of true good;[45] as long as this is so, he is plagued with the imaginations of what he has done and seen and heard, and this brings him a pleasure which he hates.

63. So it is that in both cases "their loins are filled with the

42. Gal 5:23.   43. I Tim 4:8.

44. It is not a question here of reflection on the part of the conscience to judge previous acts whether they were good or bad. It is rather simply a moment of reflection. Concupiscence (which is here understood not precisely as evil emotions and instincts but rather as unregulated attraction for sensible things, the things of this world which constantly press themselves on our senses) is not yet overcome. All the things which have caused pleasure in his senses man finds again within himself as "pleasures which charm," those which have been painful he finds as "wounds that are sore." Therefore what is considered here is not the joy of a good conscience in one case and remorse in the other.

45. William is considering here two different stages of the "animal man." In the first, concupiscence is not yet overcome, everything that comes along is allowed to enter into man's soul, even in spite of himself. In the second stage concupiscence is overcome but it is not yet totally brought into subjection. Asceticism has been seriously undertaken but one has not yet arrived at the point where he can control everything that comes in from outside; he is still drawn more or less this way and that, but he is not invaded by these things.

illusions"[46] of delights and "they are deprived of the light of their eyes"[47] which would enable them to think of spiritual things or the things of God. The man who fights against his inordinate desires is harassed by the attachments which he is not yet able completely to overcome. Whereas the man who is already on the verge of liberty cannot rid himself of the imaginations which spring from his attachments and from the harmful, distracting or idle thoughts to which they are constantly giving birth.

64. Hence it is that at the time of psalmody or prayer and other spiritual exercises the heart of God's servant, for all he refuses to admit them and struggles against them, is beset with imaginations and fantastic thoughts. Like unclean birds they perch upon him or fly round him, so that the sacrifice of his devotion is either snatched from the hand that holds it or, often, is defiled, to the extent that the offerer is reduced to tears.

65. A lamentable and wrong division is brought about in the wretched soul: while the spirit and the reason claim for themselves the heart's will and intention together with the body's prompt service, the animal nature in its insolence seizes upon the affections and the intellect so that the mind often remains without fruit.[48]

66. Hence it comes about that in weaker[49] souls and those in which the inordinate desires of the flesh and the world have not yet been perfectly mortified, ill-regulated movements of curiosity break out. So it is that unsuitable compensations for solitude and silence, quite contrary to the vocation, are sought after. Self-will seeks to indulge in stealthy turnings aside from the king's highroad of the common observances. One grabs for novelties, disgusted with the ordinary. These things seem for the moment to soothe the itch and the boredom of the sick soul as if by scratching, but in fact they irritate and kindle them, make them burn all the worse and itch all the more afterwards.

46. Ps 37:8.   47. Ps 37:11.

48. This problem of distractions recurs at all stages of the spiritual life. See below, n. 255. Cf. Exp 61, 122, 144, 178; Med 9:1.

49. *Infirmioribus*—below, n. 97, William insists on the fact that in this first stage of the spiritual life man is sick and his cell is a little infirmary.

67. Every day fresh occupations are taken up, fresh activities and fresh work are devised, different reading matter is found, not to edify the spirit[50] but to allay the boredom of a day that passes too slowly. The result is that when the solitary has rejected all that was old, all that he was accustomed to, and the attraction of the new has worn off, nothing remains but hatred of the cell and a speedy departure.

XVII. 68. For this reason devout simplicity—in religious life and solitude, the novice—lacking the guidance of reason, the attraction of love and the moderation of discretion but as it were doing violence to himself, as the potter does to the clay, needs to be shaped by a discipline of obedience as if by the hands of others and to be formed in all patience. On the wheel of obedience and in the fire of testing he must submit to the will and the judgment of his fashioner and shaper.

69. For although he may be brilliantly inventive, be skillful and endowed with outstanding intelligence, these things are the tools of vice as much as they are of virtue. Let him not then refuse to be taught to use to good advantage what he can also use to an evil end. This is precisely the work of virtue. Let inventiveness adapt the body to its purpose, let skill bring nature into shape and let intelligence make the mind not elated but a ready learner. Inventiveness, skill, intelligence and other such endowments are given freely, but it is otherwise with virtue. It would be learned with humility, sought for with hard work, possessed with love. It is worth all this, and it cannot be taught or sought or possessed in any other way.

XVIII. 70. In the first place then the newcomer to the desert must be taught to follow the teaching of the Apostle Paul and

50. *Animum*—below, n. 198, William shows how the soul which in the beginning was weak and merited the feminine name of *anima*, little by little progressing to the rational stage became more manly and took command of itself and thus became *animus*. Serious reading, well chosen, with constant application is an important element in that formation, that building up of the *animus*, as William will show when he treats of reading (n. 120 ff.).

offer up his body as a living sacrifice, consecrated to God and worthy of his acceptance, the worship due from him as a rational creature.[51] St Paul goes on to check overhasty and inquisitive examination into the things of the spirit and of God on the part of the animal man[52] in his beginner's zeal. He is as yet ignorant of the ways of God: "In virtue of the grace that is given me I warn every man who is of your company not to savor the things of God more than is due, but savor them soberly."[53]

71. Since the formation of the animal man is wholly or principally concerned with the body and the bearing of the outward man, he must be taught to deaden in accordance with reason those passions in him which belong to earth[54] and to arbitrate fairly and wisely between the claims of flesh and of spirit, which are constantly at war with one another,[55] showing favor to neither of them in his judgment.[56]

72. He must be taught to look upon his body as a sick[57] person that has been entrusted to his care; he must go against its many wishes in refusing it what is harmful to it and in forcing upon it what is profitable. He must treat it as belonging not to himself but to him by whom we have been bought at a great price in order that we may glorify him in our bodies.[58]

73. Again he must be taught to shun the reproach which the Lord levelled at his sinful people through the Prophet in the words: "You have cast me behind your bodies."[59] He must be very careful too not to allow his spirit at times to fall away in any respect from the straight path his vocation sets before him or from the dignity of his nature in order to provide for the needs or the comforts of this life, so as to do honor or show love to his body.

74. Therefore the body is to be treated strictly, so that it will not rebel or grow wanton, yet in such a way that it will be able to serve, for it has been given to the spirit to serve it. It is not to be regarded as the purpose of life but as something without which we

51. Rom 12:1.   52. 1 Cor 2:14.   53. Rom 12:3.
54. Gal 3:5.   55. Gal 5:17.   56. Rom 2:11; 1 Pet 1:17.
57. See note 49 above.   58. 1 Cor 6:20. 59. Ezek 23:35.

cannot live.[60] For we cannot break off the fellowship which we
have with the body whenever we want, but we must wait patiently
for it to be broken up in the lawful way and in the meantime
observe the conventions of a valid partnership.

XIX. We should be on such terms with it as if we had not long
to stay with it, and yet so that if things should turn out otherwise
we may not be driven to depart from it in haste.

75. This training would involve heavy labor and minute
calculations, with the danger of serious mistakes, were it not for
the common observance in all its fullness which the law of obedience
and of the cell gives to the novice once and for all.

76. Regulating his food and clothing, his work and his rest, his
silence and solitude and everything to do with the formation or the
needs of the outward man, it leaves the brother who is obedient,
patient and tranquil, free from trouble and anxiety. Its provisions
so banish and remove, once and for all, what is superfluous, so
confine what is needful within the bounds of a meet sufficiency and
an austerity within the reach of all, that there is something left for
the strong to desire while the weak need not shrink away.[61] Further
the quantity of what is allowed cannot in any respect harm the
conscience of those who avail themselves of it with thanksgiving,
and what is excluded should not cause any hardship to the body of
God's servant if it is well behaved and rightly trained.

77. In such matters, as Solomon says: "He who walks with

60. Cf. Exp 128: "In the same way, one who is God's beloved and God's
lover loves himself well and in right order if he cares for his flesh not according
to its desires but for the sake of the spirit, and if he shows charity to his spirit
in the Holy Spirit for God's sake. For we do not live for the body's sake, yet
we cannot live without the body. . . . Therefore according to the Apostle who
said: 'No man ever hates his own flesh,' it suffices not to hate the body,
although give it care we must, short of servitude to it. To the spirit, however,
the man must show charity and do honor, even to the point of complete
servitude on the part of the body. For a certain care by the spirit is owed to
the body that the body may live, but unstinted service by the body is owed to
the spirit that the spirit may wax strong; and service by both is owed to God
that the whole man may serve God."—CF 6:102–103.

61. RB 64:19.

simplicity walks confidently; but he who hardens his heart will fall into calamity."[62] For although what is necessary has been so provided for that there is no longer any room for complaint and all superfluity has been excluded, it may happen that either in public or in private something has to be added or taken away. In this case it is for the Prior[63] to decide and in obeying him his subjects will be free from all scruple and all danger.

XX. 78. The new hermit is then to be trained to follow the common observance and so bring under control the inordinate desires of his flesh by continual penance for his past life, and, in order to despise all else, to cultivate a contempt for himself.

79. He must at all times be fortified in advance against the temptations which are more savage in their assault upon the solitary who is a novice. The servant of God, who is serving God gratuitously, is unceasingly beset by vices that try to make him accept the wages they offer him in the form of pleasure.[64] This comes at the devil's suggestion, the flesh making its desires felt and the world providing material for them. The Lord our God also tempts us, to see whether we love him or not.[65] Not that he does not know and wishes to find out. It is in order that we ourselves may realize the truth more fully as a result of the temptation.

80. But it is easy to overcome and meet with reason temptations which give grounds for suspicion or at first sight are obviously evil. It is those which insinuate themselves under the appearance of good that are more difficult to recognize and more dangerous to entertain. Just as it is very difficult to observe due measure in what is believed to be good and not every desire for something good is safe.

XXI. 81. The hold, however, in which like bilge-water all temptations and evil and useless thoughts collect, is idleness. For the

---

62. Prov 10:9; 28:14.   63. RB 40:5.

64. Note the contrast: The novice comes to serve God gratuitously, and he is tempted to accept the wages of forbidden pleasure.

65. Deut 13:3.

greatest evil which can befall the mind is unemployed leisure. The servant of God should never be idle, although he is at leisure to devote himself to God. A name which gives rise to such suspicion and suggests such waste of time and such an absence of manliness must not be given to a matter of such unquestionable value, of such holiness, of such seriousness. Is leisure to devote one's time to God idleness? Rather it is the activity of all activities.[66] Anyone who in his cell is not faithful and fervent in this activity is indeed idle, whatever else he may do that is not done for the sake of this.

82. In this regard it is ridiculous to take up idle pursuits in order to avoid idleness. A pursuit is idle which either has no usefulness or does not tend to some useful purpose. The aim of activity should not be merely to pass the day more or less enjoyably or at least without becoming too weary of leisure but also that when the day is over it always leaves something in the mind that will contribute to the soul's advancement and that some fresh treasure is added each day to the heart's store.[67] A good hermit should consider that he has lost a day of his life if during the day he cannot remember having done any of the things for which a man lives in solitude.

XXII. 83. Do you ask what you are to do, with what you are to occupy yourself? First of all, after the daily sacrifice of prayer and application to reading, a part of every day should be devoted to examination of conscience and to the improvement and right ordering of the inner self.[68]

84. Then some work—even manual labor—that has been prescribed should be done, not so much for the sake of the pleasure it gives and the relaxation it affords to the mind as to preserve and nourish the taste for spiritual things. It should bring the mind some passing relaxation, but it should not dissipate it. The mind should have no difficulty in detaching itself from it as soon as it decides to

66. Cf. Exp 198: "He saw her inactive in the idle busyness or busy idleness. . . ."—CF 6:159.

67. Lk 6:45.

68. William will return to the consideration of these different exercises: examination of conscience 107; the divine office, 109ff; reading, 120ff.

return to itself, without any opposition on the part of the will clinging to it, without any contamination from the pleasure it has given or the images it leaves in the memory.

85. For man is not for the sake of woman, but woman for the sake of man.[69] It is not spiritual exercises that exist for the sake of bodily exercises but bodily for spiritual. When man was created he was provided with a helper like himself, made of man's very substance;[70] so also, physical exercise is necessary as a help to spiritual pursuits. But not all its forms are of the same value in this respect. Those are to be preferred which have the greater likeness and kinship to the spiritual; for example, meditating on something to be written or writing something to be read for spiritual edification.[71]

86. Open-air exercise and work not only distract the senses but also often exhaust the spirit, except in the case of heavy field work where great weariness of body leads to contrition and humility of heart.[72] Frequently too the tiredness it causes makes an impact which elicits stronger feelings of devotion. The same is also often seen to happen when fasts and vigils and all practices which involve affliction of the body are undertaken.

XXIII. 87. However, the serious and prudent soul[73] is ready to undertake all work and is not distracted by it but rather finds it a means to greater recollection. It always keeps in sight not so much what it is doing as the purpose of its activity and so aims at the summit of all perfection.[74] The more truly such an effort is made, the more fervently and the more faithfully is manual work done

---

69. 1 Cor 11:19.   70. Gen 2:18, 21.

71. In William's day meditation, which often involved reading or speaking aloud, and writing which was done with much more primitive tools than we have today, could well involve a considerable amount of physical output.

72. The relationship William is seeking to express here between body and soul is brought out more clearly in the Latin: *contritio corporis usque ad contritionem . . . cordis.*

73. *Animus:* See above, note 50.

74. Ps 118:96.

and all the energies of the body are brought into play.[75] The discipline imposed by good will forces the senses to concentrate: they are left without any opportunity of shaking off the weight of the work to take their pleasure, and, brought into humble subjection and service to the spirit, they are taught to adapt themselves to it both in sharing the work and in looking forward to its reward.

88. Through sin nature has abandoned due order and departed from the uprightness with which it was created. If it turns back to God it quickly recovers, in proportion to the fear and the love which it has for God, all that it lost by turning away from him. And when the spirit has begun to be formed anew to the likeness of its Creator[76] the flesh too soon takes on fresh life of its own accord[77] and begins to model itself on the reformed spirit. For even contrary to its own inclinations it begins to take delight in whatever delights the spirit. Further, because of its manifold shortcomings, the penalty of sin, it thirsts for God in many ways[78] and sometimes even attempts to outstrip its master.

89. For we do not lose our pleasures, we only transfer them from the body to the soul, from the senses to the spirit. Black bread and plain water, mere greens and vegetables are assuredly no very delectable fare: what does give great pleasure is when, for the love of Christ and the desire of interior delight, a well disciplined stomach is able to satisfy itself with such fare and be thankful. How many thousands of poor people meet the needs of nature with such things or with only one of them? Indeed it would be very easy and enjoyable to live according to nature with the love of God to season it if our folly allowed us. As soon as that is healed nature finds natural things attractive. It is the same with work: the farm laborer has strong nerves and muscular arms, the result of exercise. But if he is allowed to fall into inactivity he grows soft. The will leads to action, action induces practice, practice brings strength for all work.

75. This and other reflections make it evident that the author himself was experienced in manual labor and its relationship with the search for God and a deep interior life.

76. Col 3:10.   77. Cf. Ps 27:7.   78. Ps 62:2.

XXIV. 90. But to return to our subject. In every respect our work and our leisure should never leave us idle. Our occupation should always be that the Apostle's words to beginners and those in the animal state may find in us their perfect fulfillment: "I am speaking in human terms because nature is still strong in you. Just as you once made over your natural powers as slaves to impurity and wickedness till all was wickedness, you must now make over your natural powers as slaves to right-doing till all is sanctified."[79]

91. Let the animal man hear this. Up to the present he has been the willing slave of his body but now he is beginning to subject it to the spirit and fit himself to perceive the things of God.[80] Let him determine to shake off the yoke of so foul a servitude and rid himself of the bad habits which the flesh has imposed upon him.

92. Let him set constraint against constraint, habit against habit. Let him cultivate attachments in the place of attachments until he deserves to receive the fullness of a new enjoyment for the old enjoyment. As the Apostle recommends, may he at least take as much satisfaction in the absence of worldly and carnal pleasures as he took at first in their presence, and find as great delight in making over his natural powers as slaves to right-doing as he used to find in making them over to the service of impurity and wickedness till all was wickedness.[81]

79. Rom 6:19.   80. Mt 16:23.   81. Rom 6:19.

ADVICE FOR NOVICES

OR THIS IS THE PERFECTION OF THE
ANIMAL MAN in his state, or of the novice who is beginning. When he has reached the end of this animal or human
stage, if he does not look back, if he presses on faithfully to what lies
before him,[1] he will quickly arrive at that divine state in which
he will begin to possess as he is possessed[2] and to know as he is
known.[3] This, however, is a task that is not completed in a moment,
at a man's conversion, nor in a single day: it demands a long time
and much hard work, much sweat; it depends on God's mercy and
grace and on man's will and alacrity.[4]

XXV.   94. Now all these good practices demand the cell as their
workshop and an enduring perseverance in it.[5] In it anyone who is
on good terms with his poverty is rich;[6] whoever possesses good
will is endowed with all that he needs to live well. Yet good will is

1. Phil 3:13.   2. Phil 3:12.
3. 1 Cor 13:12. To possess God and know him as one is possessed and
known is proper to heavenly beatitude. However, already here below under
the action of the Holy Spirit something of this knowledge can be experienced.
Basically it is a question of mystical experience and in this sense William is
already here touching upon the third state, that of the spiritual man.
4. Rom 6:16.
5. RB 4:78. William is adapting here to the cell what St Benedict said of
the cloister.
6. Seneca, *Letters to Lucilius*, 4:11; trans, R. M. Gummere, *The Epistle of
Seneca*, vol. 1, Loeb Classical Series (New York: Putnam, 1934), p. 19. In
this and the following nine sections there are more than fifteen implicit

43

not always to be trusted: it must be kept in check and under control, especially in a beginner. Let the discipline of holy obedience govern good will and let good will rule the body. Let it teach the body that it can stay in one place, endure the cell and live in its own company. In one who is making progress this is the beginning of a satisfactory state of affairs and gives unmistakeable grounds for good hope.

95. For it is impossible for a man faithfully to fix his soul upon one thing who has not first perseveringly attached his body to one place. To try to escape ill-health of the soul by moving from place to place is like flying from one's own shadow. Such a man as he flies from himself carries himself with him. He changes his place, but not his soul. He finds himself the same everywhere he is, except that the constant movement itself makes him worse, just as a sick man is harmed by jolting when he is carried about.

96. Sick indeed he should know that he is, and he should give his attention to those diseased parts of himself in which his sickness lies. If he rests without disturbance the persevering application of healing measures will quickly produce their effect; the soul will be cured of its aberrations and freed from its bondage and regain complete possession of itself in God. For its nature is not merely contaminated but suffering from serious infection[7] and it needs extensive treatment. Let him stay then without moving from his infirmary (for such is the name doctors usually give to the place set apart for the healing of the sick) and continue in the course of treatment on which he has embarked until he feels himself to be cured.

XXVI. 97. Your infirmary, you who are sick and ailing, is your cell; the treatment which has begun to bring you healing is obedience, true obedience. You must know that frequent changing from

---

citations to the *Letters to Lucilius* and the whole of 102–103 is adapted from Seneca. See J. M. Déchanet, "Seneca noster, des Lettres à Lucilius à La Lettre aux Frères du Mont-Dieu" in *Mélanges de Ghellinck* (Gemblaux, 1951), pp. 753–766.

7. Seneca, *loc. cit.* 59:9; Gummere, p. 415.

one course of treatment to another is harmful; it upsets nature and weakens the sick man. For a man who is on his way to a destination will quickly arrive at it if he keeps to one road, the straight road, and so come to the end of his journey with all its toil. Whereas if he follows a multitude of roads he wanders and never comes to the end of his toil, for wandering does not lead to any end. Stay put then and do not change your course of treatment but apply the remedy of medicinal obedience until you arrive at the goal of perfect health. Do not be ungrateful either and cast it off when you are restored to health, although you may be allowed to make a different use of it thenceforward.

98. If then you wish to be cured quickly, take care not to act on your own responsibility even in the least matter, or without consulting your doctor. If you expect him to do for you what a doctor should you must never be ashamed to show him your ulcer. Be ashamed, yes, but none the less reveal everything and do not hide anything.

99. For there are some who when they confess relate the history of their sins as if they were telling a story and enumerate the ailments of their soul without any compunction, almost without any regret or any feeling of sorrow. Tears come quickly and turn into groans when sorrow is felt. But if the evil of sickness is aggravated by an insensibility which gives little ground for hope, then the lack of sorrow indicates that the nearer health seems to be the further away it is in reality.

100. But if the doctor is too gentle and wishes to cure everything by means of soothing ointments and poultices, then it is for you to take the matter into your own hands and in your eager desire for stronger and quicker measures ask for the knife, demand the cautery.

101. The doctor is always ready, and at your disposal.

XXVII. In order that your solitude may not appall you and that you may dwell the more safely in your cell three guardians have been assigned to you: God, your conscience and your spiritual father. To God you owe devotion and the entire gift of self; to your conscience the respect which will make you ashamed to sin in its presence; to your spiritual father the obedience of charity and recourse in everything.

102. In addition, to make you grateful to me, I will add a fourth and provide you with a monitor for as long as you are small and have not learned to keep the presence of God before your mind.

103. If you will take my advice, you will choose for yourself a man whose life is such that it will serve as a model to impress upon your heart, one whom you will so revere that whenever you think of him you will rise up because of the respect you feel for him and put yourself in order. Think of him as if he were present and let the charity you feel for one another act in you to correct all that needs to be corrected, while your solitude suffers no infringement of its secret. Let him be present to you whenever you wish and let him come sometimes when you would have preferred him to stay away. The thought of his holy severity will make it seem as if he were rebuking you; the thought of his kindness and goodness will bring you consolation; the purity and sanctity of his life will set you a good example. For you will be driven to correct even all your thoughts, as if they were open to his gaze and visited by his rebuke, when you consider that he is watching.

104. So, as the Apostle bids: "Keep guard on yourself"[8] with the greatest care and, in order to have your eyes always on yourself, turn your gaze away from all else. The eye is a remarkable instrument of the body—if only it could see itself as it sees other things. Now the inner eye is enabled to do this. If then it follows the example of the outward eye and neglects itself, giving its attention to the affairs of others, it will not be able to return to itself, however much it may wish to do so. Give your attention to yourself; you yourself constitute abundant matter for solicitude for yourself. Shut out also from your outward eyes what you have grown unaccustomed to see, from your inner eyes what you no longer love, since nothing so easily reasserts its claims as love, especially in younger and more tender souls.

---

8. 1 Tim 5:22.

XXVIII. 105. Make bold also to be wise at times and desire the better gifts.[9] Be yourself a parable of edification for yourself. You have one cell outwardly, another within you. The outward cell is the house in which your soul dwells together with your body; the inner cell is your conscience and in that it is God who should dwell with your spirit,[10] he who is more interior to you than all else that is within you.[11] The door of the outward enclosure is a sign of the guarded[12] door within you, so that as the bodily senses are prevented from wandering abroad by the outward enclosure so the inner senses are kept always within their own domain.

106. Love your inner cell then, love your outward cell too, and give to each of them the care which belongs to it. Let the outward cell shelter you, not hide you away; its purpose is not to let you sin without being seen but to enable you to live in greater safety. For you do not know, you, its untaught inmate, what you owe to your cell if you fail to consider not only how you are cured of your vices in it but also that you are preserved from quarrelling with people outside. You are ignorant also of the respect which you owe to your conscience if you do not in your cell experience the grace of the Holy Spirit and the joy of interior sweetness.

107. Give to each cell then the honor which is due to it and be jealous of your own primacy in it. Learn in it according to the laws of the common observance to take charge of yourself, to plan your life, set your behavior in order. Judge yourself, be your own accuser and often also condemn yourself and do not leave yourself

9. 1 Cor 12:31.

10. This comparison of the two cells is one way in which William expresses the mystery of the indwelling, the presence of God within the soul of man, in his treatise *On the Nature of the Body and the Soul.* He expresses it in another way which perhaps brings out better the vivifying activity and effect of this divine presence: "As the soul is the life of the body, so God is the life of the soul. He is its breath, and the soul aspires after him as the body aspires after air."

11. Cf. MF 19; also St Augustine, *Confessions,* 3:6; trans. J. G. Pilkington in *Basic Writings of St Augustine* (New York: Random House, 1948), p. 34.

12. *Ostium circumstantiae*—taken from Ps 140:3—signifies a certain guarded discretion or circumspection.

F

unpunished. Let justice take her seat to pass judgment[13] while conscience stands there guilty and accusing itself. No one loves you more, no one will judge you more loyally.

XXIX. 108. In the morning, demand an account of yourself for the night which is past and draw up for yourself a program for the day that lies ahead. In the evening, call a reckoning of the day which has passed and lay down a rule for the night which is coming. If you are strict in this way you will not have the leisure to seek inordinate pleasure.

109. Allot to each and every hour in accordance with the rule of the common observance its own exercises, spiritual when they are due and bodily when they are due. In this let the spirit so pay every debt to God and the body to the spirit that if anything is omitted, anything neglected, anything left unfinished, it is not allowed to go unpunished but is made up for in its own way, in its own place and at its own time.

110. In this time-table, apart from those hours of which the Prophet says: "Seven times a day have I praised you,"[14] the morning and the evening sacrifice and that of midnight are to be especially observed. For it is not without significance that the Prophet says: "In the morning I will stand before you and see."[15] He says it because at that time of day we are still free from exterior cares. Similarly he says: "Let my prayer mount like incense in your sight; the lifting up of my hands like the evening sacrifice,"[16] because by then we have more or less rid ourselves of such hindrances.

111. He indicates the same framework of witness for our nocturnal vigils also, in which we rise in the middle of the night to praise the name of the Lord,[17] when he says: "In the day of my tribulation I sought God, my hands were stretched out at night before him, or towards him, and I was not disappointed,"[18] and the rest that follows.[19]

---

13. Ps 9:5.   14. Ps 118:164.   15. Ps 5:5.
16. Ps 140:2.   17. Ps 118:62.   18. Ps 76:3.
19. Ps 76:4f: "My soul refuses to be comforted. I think of God and I moan. I meditate and my soul thinks. You hold my eyelids from closing. I am so

112. For it is at these hours especially that we ought to take our stand before God, as it were face to face,[20] and in the light of his countenance[21] see clearly, find grounds for tribulation and sorrow for ourselves in ourselves, and call upon the name of the Lord, striking sparks[22] from our spirit[23] until it bursts into flame, dwelling upon the thought of the Lord's abounding sweetness[24] until he himself makes his consolation felt in our hearts.

113. And it is then especially that we should do the Apostle's bidding: "I would rather speak five words in church which my mind utters than ten thousand which I do not understand";[25] and again: "I mean to use mind as well as spirit when I sing psalms."[26] For it is then that the mind and spirit should have their fruits gathered in, so that either we may go to rest in the quiet of the night with the abundance of God's blessing or, as we rise to sing God's praises, the whole tenor of our performance in singing those praises of God may be shaped and animated thereby.

114. Therefore in preparing for the night office it is better not to overwhelm the mind with a great number of psalms and so exhaust or extinguish the spirit. But while it is still alert it should be kindled to devotion and directed in its journey to God, until with enlarged heart it begins to run[27] and so continues until the end of the office, maintaining the pitch of its fervor unabated, unless it be undermined by some great negligence or cut off by a deliberate failing.

XXX. 115. Anyone who has the mind of Christ[28] knows also how profitable it is to Christian piety, how fitting and advantageous it is to God's servant, the servant of Christ's redemption, to devote at

---

troubled that I cannot speak. I consider the days of old, I remember the years long ago."

20. I Cor 13:12.   21. Ps 88:16.

22. The text had originally *scabendo* but it was corrected to *scobendo*, undoubtedly to follow the text of Cassian: *Conferences,* 1:19 (Cistercian Studies Series 20). See CG 5 and note 32 there, CF 3:41.

23. Ps 76:7.   24. Ps 144:7.   25. I Cor 14:19.

26. I Cor 14:15.   27. Ps 118:32; RB Prol. 49.   28. I Cor 2:16.

least one hour of the day to an attentive passing in review of the benefits conferred by his Passion and the Redemption he wrought, in order to savor them in spirit and store them away faithfully in the memory. This is spiritually to eat the Body of the Lord and drink his Blood in remembrance of him who gave to all who believe in him the commandment: "Do this in remembrance of me."[29]

116. Quite apart from the sin of disobedience it is obvious to everyone how impious it would be for a man to be mindless of such great loving-kindness on the part of God, since it is a crime to forget a friend who at his departure left a memorial of himself in whatever form.

117. Now only a few men who have been entrusted with this ministry are allowed to celebrate, in the proper way and place and at the proper time, the mystery of this holy and venerable commemoration.[30] But the substance of the mystery[31] can be enacted and handled and received for salvation at all times and in every place where God rules,[32] in the way in which it was given, that is, with due sentiments of devotion, by all those to whom are addressed the words: "You are a chosen race, a royal priesthood, a consecrated nation, a people God means to have for himself; it is yours to proclaim the exploits of the God who has called you out of darkness into his marvellous light."[33]

---

29. Lk 22:19.

30. William is here speaking of the holy sacrifice of the Mass as it is offered by one who has been ordained to the ministerial priesthood.

31. "Substance of the mystery—*Rem mysterii.* William here contrasts *mysterium* and *res mysterii.* The former refers to the external rite without however excluding the inner reality; the latter refers to the inner reality itself. The distinction is not foreign to that which would be clearly made later by the scholastics who would speak of *res* and *sacramentum* (the Greek word *mystérion* is translated by both "mystery" and by "sacrament").

32. Ps 102:22. This is just another way of saying everywhere. In his treatise *On the Nature and Dignity of Love,* William, in order to express the idea that one should pray everywhere, writes: "Every place where God exercises his supreme dominion ought to be a place of prayer." (NDL 25).

33. 1 Pet 2:9.

118. As for the sacrament, while it brings life to one who receives it worthily, it can be profaned by an unworthy reception, and then it brings death and judgment. But the substance of the sacrament[34] is only received by the man who is worthy of it and duly prepared. The sacrament without its substance brings death to the communicant; but the substance of the sacrament, even without the visible species, brings eternal life.

119. Now if you wish, and if you truly desire it, this is at your disposal in your cell at all hours both of day and of night. As often as you stir up sentiments of piety and faith in recalling to mind what he did when he suffered for you, you eat his body and drink his blood. As long as you remain in him through love and he in you through the sanctity and justice he works in you, you are reckoned as belonging to his Body and counted as one of his members.

XXXI. 120. Next, at fixed hours time should be given to certain definite reading. For haphazard reading, constantly varied and as if lighted upon by chance does not edify but makes the mind unstable;[35] taken into the memory lightly, it goes out from it even more lightly.[36] But you should concentrate on certain authors and let your mind grow accustomed to them.

121. The Scriptures need to be read and understood in the same spirit in which they were written. You will never enter into Paul's meaning until by constant application to reading him and by giving yourself to constant meditation you have imbibed his spirit. You will never understand David until by experience you have made the very sentiments of the psalms your own. And that

34. See above, n. 31.

35. We have seen above (n. 66, note 50) that serious and assiduous reading is one of the factors which builds up ("edifies") the *animus*—the mind or spirit.

36. Memory for William is not simply the faculty which remembers, rather it is that part of the soul where all the knowledge coming into it from outside is gathered together and where all thoughts are elaborated. See R. Thomas, *Notes sur Guillaume de St-Thierry* (Pain de Cîteaux, 2, Chambarand, 1959), pp. 11f.

applies to all Scripture. There is the same gulf between attentive study and mere reading as there is between friendship and acquaintance with a passing guest, between boon companionship and chance meeting.

122. Some part of your daily reading should also each day be committed to memory, taken in as it were into the stomach, to be more carefully digested and brought up again for frequent rumination; something in keeping with your vocation and helpful to concentration, something that will take hold of the mind and save it from distraction.

123. The reading should also stimulate the feelings and give rise to prayer, which should interrupt your reading: an interruption which should not so much hamper the reading as restore to it a mind ever more purified for understanding.

124. For reading serves the purpose of the intention with which it is done. If the reader truly seeks God in his reading, everything that he reads tends to promote that end,[37] making the mind surrender in the course of the reading and bring all that is understood into Christ's service.[38] But if the intention of the reader is directed elsewhere, it draws everything in its wake and nothing that it finds in Scripture is too holy or too religious not to be applied to its own perverseness or folly, through the pursuit of vainglory or a distortion of meaning or a wrong understanding. For all the Scriptures demand that the reader should approach them in the fear of the Lord. In that fear, first of all he should make his intention steadfast, and then from it should derive all his understanding and appreciation of what he reads and the proper ordering of it.

XXXII. 125. Spiritual exercises should never be laid aside in favor of bodily ones for any length of time nor totally, but the mind should learn to return to them easily and give itself to bodily exercises while still being attached to the things of the spirit.[39] For

37. Cf. Rom 8:28.   38. 2 Cor 10:5.

39. Concerning the relative value of bodily exercises or external observances, see Apo 12ff., pp. 46ff.

as has already been said[40] it is not man who is for the sake of woman but woman for the sake of man[41] and it is not spiritual things that are for the sake of carnal but carnal that are for the sake of spiritual. By bodily exercises in the present context we mean those which involve manual work.

126. There are also other exercises at which the body must toil, such as vigils, fasts and the like, which are no hindrance to spiritual things but help them if they are done with reason and discretion. If, however, through the vice of indiscretion they are practiced in such a way that either the spirit grows faint or the body is enfeebled and so spiritual things are hampered, the man who so behaves cheats his body of the effects of good work, his spirit of its affections, his neighbor of good example and God of honor. He is guilty of sacrilege and responsible to God for all this damage.

127. Not that, to follow the Apostle's teaching, it is not in keeping with human nature[42] or unfitting or undue or unjust to have an occasional headache in God's service, when the pursuit of worldly vanity has previously brought on many a headache. Similarly with a hunger that the stomach feels to the extent of audible protest; it was often stuffed to the point of vomiting. But in all things due measure should be observed. The body should be mortified at times, but not broken. For even bodily training is of some value, not very great, but nonetheless useful.[43]

128. Therefore some care should be taken of the flesh, that is to say to such an extent as will not foster inordinate desires. This care should be moderate and display a certain spiritual discipline, so that nothing may appear in its manner or its quality or its quantity that is not fitting to God's servant.

129. For what seems base in us we should surround with special honor, while what is seemly in us has no such need.[44] And further we should present the whole of our life, however hidden it may be from men, holy and honorable before God. All our behavior should

---

40. See above, n. 85.   41. 1 Cor 11: 9.   42. Rom 6:19.

43. Cf. 1 Tim 4:8.   44. 1 Cor 12:23f.

be such as the holy angels may look upon with pleasure although it is confined within the walls of our own dwelling.

130. "Let all that you do," says the Apostle, "be done with modesty."[45] Modesty is something that pleases God and is loved by the holy angels. It is for this reason that the Apostle also bids women to cover themselves "on account of the angels."[46] Without any doubt they are always with you in your cells, keeping guard over you, rejoicing in your efforts and assisting them; they are pleased if, although there is no man to see, all that you do is done with modesty.[47]

XXXIII. 131. So whether you eat or drink or do anything else, do everything in the name of the Lord, devoutly, reverently and religiously.[48]

132. If you eat, let your sobriety lend its adornment to a table which is already sparing. And when you eat do not give yourself wholly to the business of eating. While the body is securing its refreshment let not the mind wholly neglect its own but dwell upon and as it were digest something that it recalls of the Lord's sweetness or a passage from the Scriptures that will feed it as it meditates upon it or at least remembers it. The bodily need itself should be satisfied not in a worldly or carnal way but as befits a monk and is becoming to God's servant. Even from the point of view of health, the more becoming and orderly the manner of eating, the easier and more wholesome is the process of digestion.

133. Watch must be kept then on the manner and the time of eating, on the quality and the quantity of the food; all superfluity and seasonings that only adulterate food should be shunned.

134. Watch must be kept on the manner, so that the eater does

---

45. 1 Cor 16:14.   46. 1 Cor 11:10.

47. The early Cistercians were very conscious of the angels. St Bernard has written so extensively on them, especially the guardian angels, that he is said to be the Doctor of the Angels. See his *Sermons On the Song of Songs* (Cistercian Fathers Series 3, 7, 31, 40), especially *Sermon Nineteen* and the *Sermons on Psalm 90* (Cistercian Fathers Series 13).

48. 1 Cor 10:31.

not pour out his soul over everything he eats; watch on the time, lest the hour be anticipated; on the quality, which should be that of the community's food except when obvious infirmity demands something better. As regards seasoning let it be enough, I beg, that our food be edible, not also such as to provoke appetite or tickle the palate. Appetite contains enough disorder of itself; it can scarcely or not at all satisfy its needs without the accompaniment of some enjoyment and if it begins to receive stimulants from men who have declared an unending war on its enticements, it is two against one and temperance is endangered.

XXXIV. 135. Next, the same applies to sleep as has been said about food. Take care, servant of God, as far as you can, never to give yourself wholly to sleep, lest your sleep be not the rest of a weary man but the entombment of a stifled body; not the refreshment but the extinction of your spirit. Sleep is something of which to be watchful. To a great extent it resembles drunkenness. Apart from vice (which meets with no opposition in one who is asleep, since the reason shares the body's suspension of activity), in regard to the duty of making continual progress no space of time is so utterly wasted in our life as that which is given to sleep.

136. Accordingly when you go to sleep always take with you in your memory or your thoughts something that will enable you to fall asleep peacefully and sometimes even help you to dream; something also that will come to mind when you wake up and renew in you the previous day's purpose. In this way light will be shed on the night for you and it will be as the day, and the night will be your illumination in your delights.[49] You will fall asleep peacefully, you will rest in tranquillity, you will wake up easily and when you rise you will have no difficulty in returning with your wits about you to what you have not wholly laid aside.

137. For temperate food and moderation of the senses are followed by undisturbed sleep.[50] But carnal and bestial sleep, a

---

49. Ps 138:11f. Cf. Exp 187, CF 6:151–152.

50. *Sobrium enim cibum sobriumque sensum, sequitur sobrius somnus.* William in his *Life of St Bernard* presents him as a model in this, LSB 21f.

Lethean sleep,[51] should be an object of abhorrence to God's servant. From temperate sleep it is easy after a suitable period of repose to recall the senses both of body and of mind, arousing them and setting them to work like the servants of a well-ordered household to do whatever tasks are required by the spirit. Such sleep at the right time and in the right manner is not to be scorned.

138. Indeed the prudent soul which is dedicated to God should behave in its cell and in its conscience in the same way as the master of a household in his home. He should not have in his house, to quote Solomon, "a quarrelsome woman"[52]—his flesh. It should be trained to temperance and ready for obedience and work; taught to be hungry and to be filled as the occasion may demand, to have plenty and to be in want.[53] His outer senses should not be his rulers but his servants, his inner senses sober and active. The whole household or family of his thoughts should be so marshaled and disciplined that when he tells one of them to go it goes and another to come, he comes, and when he bids his servant the body to do so and so he does it without arguing.[54]

139. The man who so governs and disposes himself in his conscience can be left to himself in his cell with complete security. But this is for the perfect or for those who are making progress in a perfect way, and if we set it before beginners and novices it is in order that they may know what is lacking to them[55] and at what their efforts should aim.

---

51. Virgil, *Aeneid* 6:714, trans. H. R. Fairclough, Loeb Classical Series (New York: Putnam, 1920) vol. 1, p. 555. The Lethe was one of the rivers of the underworld, whose waters according to mythology induced in the drinker a forgetfulness.

52. Prov 21:9; 25:24.   53. Phil 4:12.   54. Mt 8:9.   55. Ps 38:5.

VOCATIONS—POVERTY—SELF-SUPPORT

IT SHOULD BE NOTED that when we speak of carnal or animal perception, of rational knowledge or of spiritual wisdom, we have in mind both a single man, in whom according to various degrees of progress and advancement and differing intensities of fervor all these can be found at one time or another, and three kinds of men, each of whom engages in the combat of the religious life in the cell in accord with the characteristics of one of these states.

141. Yet the dignity of a cell and the secret of holy solitude and the name of "solitary" would seem to be only for the perfect, who feed, as the Apostle says, on solid food and whose faculties are so trained by exercise that they can distinguish between good and evil.[1] The rational man, who is near to being a wise man, might seem to be tolerated there, but the animal man who does not perceive the things of God[2] it would seem should be wholly excluded.

142. But we are faced with the Apostle Peter who says[3] of certain people: "If they received the Holy Spirit just as we did, who was I to stay God's hand?"[4] For the Holy Spirit is good will. And it is not without great hesitation that anyone is to be excluded from

1. Heb 5:14.   2. 1 Cor 11:14.

3. St Peter said this of the centurian Cornelius and all the members of his household who with him received an outpouring of the Holy Spirit when Peter preached to them. See Acts 10.

4. Acts 11:17.

57

any vocation, to whatever heights it aspires, whose good will bears
witness to the indwelling and the attraction of the Holy Spirit.

143. In fact cells are to be peopled with two kinds of men:
either with the simple who in their hearts and their good will seem
to possess the fervor and the ability to arrive at religious prudence;
or with the prudent who are proved to be eager for religious and
holy simplicity. But foolish pride or proud folly should always be
kept away from the tents of the just.[5] Now all pride is foolish,
although not all folly is proud. For foolishness without pride is
sometimes found to be simplicity, and if it is ignorant it can
perhaps be taught; and if it cannot be taught it may perhaps be
formed by careful treatment.

144. Religious life in common is the proper city of refuge[6] for
simplicity, unless it is such that it refuses to be humiliated or
so wild that it cannot be governed or formed.

However, good will, even though it may be very wild, should
not be abandoned but by means of wholesome guidance be
brought to a life of activity and exertion. But when it is proud,
however prudent it may seem to be to itself, it should be left to its
own devices and sent away. For if a proud man is admitted, on the
very day on which he comes in to take up his abode he begins to
lay down the law, truly too stupid to learn the laws he finds
already in force.

145. Admission to living with oneself[7] should then be a matter
for careful and prudent deliberation. For the man who lives with
himself has with him only himself, such as he is. It is never safe for a
bad man to live with himself, because he is living with a bad man

---

5. Ps 117:15.

6. Num 35:9. Aelred of Rievaulx also speaks of these "cities of refuge" in
relation to the monastic life. He sees these six cities of refuge spoken of in the
thirty-fifth chapter of the Book of Numbers as representing the six general
exercises of the monastic life: three corporal: work, watching and fasting; and
three spiritual: reading, prayer and meditation.—Third Sermon for the Feast of
St Benedict, 11ff; trans. M. B. Pennington in *Cistercian Studies* 4 (1969), pp.
86f.

7. Cf. Gregory the Great, *Dialogues*, 2:3 (PL 66:36) where St Gregory uses
the same expression to describe St Benedict's solitary life at Subiaco.

and no one gives him more trouble than he himself does. The insane, those distraught with grief and those who for any reason are not in full possession of their minds are usually kept under guard and not left to themselves, so that they may not turn their solitude to ill account.

146. Men in the animal state who are humble and poor in spirit[8] may then be admitted to the company of those who dwell in cells, but with the aim that they may become rational and spiritual, not that on their account those who have already attained to such a state should turn back and be made animal again. Let them be received with all kindness and charity, borne with in all patience and indulgence. But the compassion shown to them should not lead anyone to model himself on them, neither should anyone so seek their progress that because of them he is forced to fall away from the strictness he had resolved upon in his religious life.

XXXVI. 147. For so it comes about that with money that does not belong to us the building of costly and, insofar as very shame allows, imposing cells is undertaken. We abandon that holy rusticity which, as Solomon says,[9] was created by the Most High and we create for ourselves dwelling-places which display a sort of religious respectability. In these such compassion is shown to men in the animal state that we have almost all been made animal in this respect.

148. Banishing from ourselves and from our cells the pattern of poverty and the model of holy simplicity, the true beauty of God's house, bequeathed to us by our Fathers, we build for ourselves by the hands of skilled craftsmen cells which are not so much eremitic

---

8. Mt 5:3.

9. Sir 7:16. William's kindness and delicacy is evident here where as he reproaches the Carthusians he identifies with them using the first person plural, "we." There is no doubt, as is very evident from his description of the Golden Age of Clairvaux (LSB 35), that William was very much in sympathy with the Cistercian's love for poverty and simplicity and was the very pleased recipient of Bernard of Clairvaux's colorful satire rebuking the Cluniacs' failures in this respect. See Apo 16ff, CF 1:52ff.

as aromatic,[10] each of them costing a hundred golden pieces. They are the delight of our eyes[11] but they come from the alms of the poor.[12]

149. Take away, Lord, the reproach[13] of these hundred golden pieces from the cells of your poor men. Why not rather a hundred copper coins?[14] Why not rather nothing at all? Why do not the sons of grace rather build for themselves free of cost?[15] What was the answer given to Moses when he was completing the Tabernacle? "See," he was told, "that you make everything according to the model that was shown to you on the mountain."[16]

150. Is it right that the place where God dwells with men[17] should be made by men of the world? Let it be themselves, they to whom is shown in the heights of their spirit the model of the true beauty of God's house, let it be themselves who do their own building. Let it be themselves, they who are bidden by their preoccupation with interior things to scorn and disregard all outward things, let it be themselves who do their own building. No skill on the part of hired craftsmen will be so successful as their own lack of concern in producing an expression of poverty, the beauty of holy simplicity and the traditional sobriety of the Fathers.

XXXVII. 151. I beg you therefore, while we are pilgrims in this world and soldiers on earth,[18] let us not build for ourselves houses to settle down in but make tents we can leave at a moment's notice, we who are liable to be called away from them in the near future to our fatherland and our own city, to the home where we shall spend our eternity.[19] We are in camp, we are campaigning in a foreign country. Whatever is natural is easy, but in a strange land hard work is the rule. Is it not easy for a solitary and enough for nature and in keeping with conscience to weave for himself a cell

10. Cf. Exp 194, CF 6:155–157.   11. Ezek 24:21.

12. Cf. Apo 28, CF 1:63–66.   13. Ps 118:39.

14. Literally "a hundred denarii"—the sum owed by the fellow servant to the forgiven but unforgiving servant in the parable of the Lord: Mt 18:28.

15. Cf. Mt 17:26.   16. Ex 25:40.   17. Rev 21:3.

18. Job 7:1.   19. Sir 12:5.

out of pliant boughs, plaster it with mud, cover it with anything that comes to hand and so come by a dwelling-place eminently suited to him? What more could be desired?[20]

152. Take it on faith, brethren, and God grant you may not learn by experience that these works of art, this imposing exterior are quick to slacken a manlike determination and tend to make the masculine spirit effeminate.[21] For although the pleasure they give often ceases with use, although there may be some who use such things as if they were not using them,[22] yet attachments of this kind are rooted out and vanquished more effectively by contempt than by use.

153. For what is within us is benefited in no slight degree by what is around us, when it is arranged to accord with our minds and in its own way to correspond with the ideals we have set before us. For poorer surroundings check ill-ordered desires in some people, in others they awaken the conscience to love of poverty.

154. And again, a spirit that is intent on interior things is better served by an absence of decoration and trimming in the things around it. Although such men live in a house, they show that they have their minds elsewhere most of the time, and the holy purpose which they pursue declares that their preoccupations are of another order. The interior life is effectively brought into harmony with a good conscience when all externals are proclaimed to be of little value.

155. I beg then that, while those elegant cells remain as they have been made, no addition be made to their number. Let them serve as infirmaries for brethren in the animal state and as yet sick, until they regain their health, that is, begin to desire not infirmaries for sick men but the tents of those who are on campaign in the

20. A parallel passage is found in the Homily of St John Chrysostom on Chapter Twelve of St Matthew's Gospel, n. 3 (PG 58:651) which is read by the Carthusians on the Feast of St Bruno.

21. The *animus* of the rational man returns to being the *anima* of the animal man. See above, n. 147.

22. 1 Cor 7:31.

camps of the Lord. Let them remain also as an example to those who
come after you, so that they may see that when you possessed such
cells you scorned them.

XXXVIII. 156. But you who are spiritual,[23] like the Hebrews,
that is, men of passage, not having here a lasting city but in quest of
one that lies in the future,[24] build yourselves, as you did in the
beginning, huts to live in. For it was in huts that our Fathers[25]
lived when they lived in the land of promise as in a foreign country,
looking forward, together with the heirs of the promise, to the city
which has true foundations, whose founder and designer is God.[26]
They did not receive the fulfillment of the promises but welcomed
them at a distance, owning themselves no better than strangers and
pilgrims on earth. For men who speak like this make it clear
enough that the country of their desires is a better, heavenly
country.[27]

157. For the same reason our Fathers in Egypt and the Thebaid,
in their burning zeal for this holy way of life, dwelling in solitary
places, enduring hardship and distress, men of whom the world was
not worthy,[28] built cells for themselves which simply gave them
shelter and protection from wind and rain. In such dwellings they
abounded in the delights of eremitic austerity and in their poverty
enriched many.[29]

158. I am at a loss to find a name worthy of them; shall I call
them heavenly men or earthbound angels? They lived on earth but
their true home was in heaven.[30] They worked with their own
hands and fed the poor with the fruits of their toil. While they
themselves went hungry they contributed food from the wastes of
the desert to feed the prisons and the hospitals of cities and succored
those who were laboring under any form of distress. Yet all this

---

23. Gal 6:1.   24. Heb 13:14.

25. The Fathers referred to here seem to be Abraham and the Patriarchs.
See J. M. Déchanet, *Lettre d'Or,* p. 172, note 170.

26. Heb 11:10.   27. Heb 11:13f.   28. Heb 11:38.

29. 2 Cor 6:10   30. Phil 3:20.

time they lived by the work of their own hands and dwelt in buildings their own hands had erected.

XXXIX. 159. What is there left for us to say?[31] We are not animal men but earthly animals, clinging to the earth and to the senses of our flesh, living according to the dictates of the flesh, depending upon others for our livelihood.

160. As regards that, however, we can find some slight consolation in the example of him who although he was rich became poor for our sakes[32] and laid down the commandment of voluntary poverty, while he himself deigned to show us an example of the same poverty in his own life. For in order to teach those who embrace the poverty of the Gospel what they have to do, he also chose to be fed by the faithful and sometimes even did not refuse to accept the necessaries of life from infidels,[33] but then it was in order to make them believers.

161. In the early Church too, as we learn from the Acts of the Apostles and St Paul's Epistles,[34] the Apostles showed the greatest solicitude and tender care in ensuring that the faithful should support those poor members of the church who for Christ's sake had suffered the loss of all their property[35] or in accordance with the counsels of perfection[36] had left or sold everything and given it to the community of the faithful, their brethren.[37]

162. There is no question that this privilege is to be conceded to the preachers of the Gospel, for our Lord gave the command that it should be so.[38] But we have the Apostles' authority for granting it also to those who live according to the Gospel, like those holy poor people who were then in Jerusalem and were called the holy poor for this very reason that they had made profession of holiness and the common life, freely impoverishing themselves to that end.

163. It is true that the Apostle shows the utmost severity in instructing certain persons that "the man who refuses to work

31. Rom 8:31.   32. 2 Cor 8:9.   33. Lk 5:29; 15:2; 19:2ff.
34. Acts 4:35; 9:29; 1 Cor 16:1ff; 2 Cor 8f.   35. Heb 10:34.
36. Lk 12:33; 18:22.   37. Acts 2:44f.   38. 1 Cor 9:14.

G

must be left to starve,"³⁹ but he immediately makes it clear whom he has in mind when he goes on to say: "We are told that there are those among you who make themselves a nuisance and live in idleness, neglecting their own business to mind other people's. We charge all such, we appeal to them in the Lord Jesus Christ, to earn their own bread by going on calmly with their work."⁴⁰ When he says "their own bread" he means bread earned by their own work. Yet he is clearly unwilling to shame or reject those who, however troublesome, however idle, however neglectful of their own business to mind other people's, have none the less the Lord's name invoked upon them,⁴¹ for he goes on at once to say: "For yourselves, brethren, never weary of doing good in Christ Jesus our Lord."⁴² As if to say: Even though they continue in their inactivity, do you none the less not grow weary of supporting them by your alms.

XL. 164. Therefore since he had previously declared with the utmost severity that those who refuse to work must be left to starve, and then shortly after showed himself somewhat milder towards those who do no work, we might say, keeping to the letter of his declaration and without seeming to run counter to the truth, that his severity was directed against those who refused to work although they were well able to do so, while he showed indulgence to those who were willing to work but quite unable. However, since he tells these latter also and begs them in the Lord Jesus Christ to eat their own bread in silence, they would seem not to be eating their own bread if they do not make it their own by working to the extent that they are able to work, as God and their conscience bear witness.

165. Pardon, Lord, pardon. We invent excuses and find pretexts, but there is no one who can hide from the light of your truth,⁴³

39. 2 Thess 3:10.   40. 2 Thess 3:11f.

41. A biblical expression taken from the Old Testament to indicate that one belonged to the people of God or the chosen people (e.g. Sir 36:14). This is also found in the New Testament (Acts 15:17).

42. 2 Thess 3:15.   43. Ps 18:7.

which not only enlightens the converted but also strikes those who turn away. Not even the bones you made to be hidden within men are hidden from you.[44] And yet we make them hidden to ourselves, for there is scarcely anyone who, in those things which concern you, is willing to make trial of what he can do. But that he finds it possible to do, without the least hesitation, whenever it is a question of worldly or carnal things and he is either driven by fear or drawn by cupidity. But even if we deceive men who do not know us, do not allow us, as if attempting to deceive you, to deceive ourselves. We do not work because either we are not able, or we seem to ourselves to be unable, or we have made ourselves unable by growing accustomed to leisure and enjoying our pleasures.[45]

XLI.   166. Let us then always worship you and fall down and weep before you who created us[46] and made us what we are by our own manifest sin and your own hidden judgment. Perhaps it is because we have no great inclination that we are unable; or because we refused to do it when we were able we are now unable when we are willing. Let us at least eat our bread in accordance with the penalty inflicted on Adam. If we cannot in the sweat of our brow,[47] then in the pain of our heart; with tears of sorrow if we cannot with the sweat that accompanies work. Let this great deficit in the way we live our profession be made up for by piety and the devotion of a humbled conscience. Let our tears be our bread day and night as long as our soul is asked: "Where is your God?"[48] that is, as long as it is on pilgrimage far away from the Lord its God[49] and from the light of his face.[50]

167. One thing only was necessary,[51] but in what class shall we

44. Ps 138:15.

45. William employs here the "we" form including in his thought himself as much as the Carthusians. We know in actual fact that one of the things that motivated his change from the Black Monks to White Monks of Cîteaux was a desire to be able to participate in one of the basic monastic exercises, that of manual labor. However, age and failing health soon deprived him of this consolation as he notes above in the Prefatory Letter, nn. 7 and 14.

46. Ps 94:6.	47. Gen 2:17ff.	48. Ps 41:4.
49. 2 Cor 5:6.	50. Ps 88:16.	51. Lk 10:42.

be reckoned who are neither stable in one thing nor practiced in many? Would that it might be with him of whom the Apostle says: "The man who does not work but believes in him who justifies the impious has his faith reckoned as justice according to God's gracious plan."[52] Would that it might be with that sinful woman who was forgiven much because she loved much.[53] And blessed is the soul which deserves to obtain justification with God through such a judgment, the judgment of them that love the name of the Lord,[54] so that without any justice deriving from works or any confidence based on merits it may be justified by the sole fact that it has loved much. For in loving you, God, the conscience which loves finds great reward in the love itself which it has for you, and also it obtains eternal life.

168. So, brethren, I beg, let us not excuse but rather accuse ourselves and make confession. And let us who rest in the shadow of a great name[55] and wear as it were the mask of perfection in the sight of men, recognize the poverty of our conscience in the sight of God and not depart wholly from the truth, so that the truth may set us free.[56]

---

52. Rom 4:5.   53. Lk 7:47.   54. Ps 118:132.
55. Lucan, *De bello civili*, 1:135; trans. J. D. Duff, Loeb Classical Series (New York: Putnam, 1928), p. 13.
56. Jn 8:32.

PRAYER

NEXT THE BEGINNER in the animal state, Christ's raw recruit, should be taught also to draw near to God so that God in turn may draw near to him. For such is the Prophet's exhortation: "Draw near to God and he will draw near to you."[1] Man has not only to be created and formed but also endowed with life. For first God formed man, then he breathed into his face the breath of life, so that man became a living soul.[2] The formation of a man is his moral training, his life is the love of God.

170. This is conceived by faith, brought forth by hope, formed and endowed with life by charity, that is, the Holy Spirit.[3] For the love of God, or the Love that is God, the Holy Spirit, infusing itself into man's love and spirit, attracts him to itself;[4] then God loves himself in man and makes him, his spirit and his love, one with himself. For as the body has no means of living apart from its spirit, so man's affections, which are called love, have no means of living, that is to say, of loving God, but the Holy Spirit.

171. Now the love of God in man which is born of grace is fed

---

1. Jas 4:8.   2. Gen 2:7.

3. William here adheres to what was at his time not an uncommon opinion namely that charity was not something created in the soul but was the Holy Spirit himself dwelling there. This is the position which was held by Peter Lombard in his *Sentences* (Book One, Dist. 17) and which was refuted by Thomas Aquinas in his *Summa Theologiae* (II–II, q. 23, art. 2).

4. *Afficit eum sibi.* In regards to this expression see CG 7, note 69; 11, note 107; CF 3:47 and 53.

with the milk of reading, nourished with the food of meditation, strengthened and enlightened by prayer.

The best and safest reading matter and subject for meditation for the animal man, newly come to Christ, to train him in the interior life, is the outward actions of our Redeemer. In them he should find an example of humility, a stimulant to charity and to sentiments of piety. Likewise from the Sacred Scriptures and the writings of the holy Fathers it is those parts which deal with morality and are easier to understand that should be put before him.

172. He should also be given the lives of the saints and the accounts of their martyrdoms. He should not trouble himself with historical details but should always find something to stir his novice's mind to love God and despise himself. The reading of other narratives gives pleasure but does not edify. Rather they distract the mind and at the time of prayer and meditation cause all manner of useless or harmful thoughts to surge up from the memory. The nature of the reading determines the quality of the subsequent meditation. The reading of difficult works tires the unpracticed mind instead of refreshing it. It shatters its powers of concentration and dulls its understanding.

XLIII. 173. The novice should also be taught to raise his heart on high in his prayer, to pray spiritually, to keep as far away as he can from material objects or their representations when he thinks of God.[5] He should be exhorted to direct his attention with all the purity of heart which he can muster to him to whom he is offering the sacrifice of his prayer, to advert to himself, the offerer, and to appreciate what he is offering and what is its quality. For to the extent that he sees or understands him to whom he is making his offering, he reaches out to him with his affections, and love itself is understanding for him.[6] And to the extent that this love animates

5. William has moved ahead very rapidly here and is already proposing to the novice a state of prayer which belongs to the spiritual man. See Exp 19, CF 6:14.

6. *Amor ipse intellectus est*—this is a favorite concept of William's to which he will return again in this epistle and frequently brings up in his other writings. See above, Introduction, pp. xxviiff; also Exp 57, note 18, CF 6:46.

his affections, he realizes that his offering is worthy of God, and so all is well with him.

174. Yet it is better and safer, as has been said already, to put before such a man when he is praying or meditating a representation of our Lord's humanity—of his birth, passion and resurrection—so that the weak spirit which is only able to think of material objects and their properties may have something to which it can apply itself and cling with devout attention, as befits its degree. Christ presents himself in his character of Mediator, and as such, as we read in Job: "The man who contemplates his own form does not sin."[7] When the novice concentrates his powers upon him, thinking of God in a human form, he does not wholly depart from the truth, so that as long as his faith does not separate God from man he will learn eventually to grasp God in man.[8]

175. In this matter those who are poorer in spirit and more simple sons of God find as a rule that at first their feelings are the sweeter the nearer they are to human nature. Afterwards however, when faith becomes a movement of love, and they embrace Christ Jesus in the midst of their hearts with love's sweet embrace, wholly man because of the human nature he took to himself, wholly God because it was God who took the nature, they begin to know him no longer according to the flesh,[9] although they are not yet fully able to conceive of him in his divinity. And enthroning him in their hearts[10] they love to offer him the vows which their lips have uttered:[11] supplications, prayers, entreaties, in keeping with the time and the matter.

7. Job 5:24. Cf. this passage with Exp 16f. where William refers to the same text from Job.

8. Cf. the Christmas Preface which calls upon us to see God physically in man and through this to pass on to love of the invisible.

9. 2 Cor 5:16. Cf. Med 10:4ff. This same doctrine concerning the role of the sacred humanity of Christ according to the flesh leading up to a knowledge of Christ according to the spirit is developed by Bernard of Clairvaux in Sermon 20:6ff., *On the Song of Songs* (Cistercian Fathers Series 4). See J. M. Déchanet, "La Christologie de St Bernard" in *St Bernard Théologien* (Rome: Editions Cisterciens, 1954) pp. 78–91.

10. 1 Pet 3:5.   11. Ps 65:13f.

XLIV. 176. For some prayers are short and simple, as they are formed by the will or the need of the one who is praying to meet the requirements of the moment. Others are longer and more intellectual, as in search of truth, asking, seeking, knocking until they receive, find and the door is opened to them.[12] Others are winged, proceeding from the spirit and bearing rich fruit, expressing the affections which accompany fruition and the joy of illuminating grace.[13] The Apostle enumerates these kinds of prayer in a different order: supplications, prayers, petitions and thanksgiving.[14]

177. Petition is what we put in the first place and it is concerned with obtaining temporal benefits and what is necessary for this life. When a man makes petition God indeed approves his good will but he follows his own better judgment and enables the one who makes petition in the right spirit to acquiesce in his will. It is of this that the Psalmist says: "My prayer is still for what pleases them."[15] That is to say, what pleases even godless men, for all men alike, but especially the sons of this world,[16] desire the tranquillity of peace, bodily health, good weather and what else contributes to a right use of this life and the satisfying of its needs, even indeed what serves the pleasure of those who make ill use of life. Those who in faith make their petitions for these intentions, although they only ask for them to meet their needs, none the less always submit their will in this respect too to the will of God.

178. Supplication is a troubled and insistent turning to God

---

12. Mt 7:7f.

13. "Illuminating grace" is the light which accompanies and indeed brings about the mystical experience. The soul is created in God's image (triune having memory, understanding, and will and one, being of one substance). In its potency to know and love God, it is the image of God by created grace (cf. Exp 22, 174). Under the supernatural illumination of grace the soul can progressively (as it could normally and easily before the original sin) know and love God. It is then made to the image of God by illuminating grace. William speaks very frequently in his works of this illuminating grace; see especially the Analytic Index of Exp under "illuminating grace," CF 6:166.

14. 1 Tim 2:1.   15. Ps 140:5.   16. Lk 16:8.

during one's spiritual exercises, in which to add fresh knowledge before grace comes to the assistance is to add fresh pain.[17]

179. Prayer is the affection of a man who clings to God, a certain familiar and devout conversation, a state in which the enlightened mind enjoys God as long as it is permitted.

180. Thanksgiving is an unwearying and undistracted attention of the good will to God in understanding and knowledge of God's grace, even if sometimes outward activity or interior affection is either non-existent or sluggish. It is of this that the Apostle says: "Praiseworthy intentions are always ready to hand, but I cannot find my way to the performance of them."[18] As if to say: good will indeed is always present, but at times it is ineffective because although I seek to perform some good work I do not find the means.

This is charity, which never fails.[19]

181. It is the uninterrupted prayer or thanksgiving of which the Apostle says: "Pray without interruption and give thanks at all times."[20] For it is a certain unchanging goodness of the mind and of the well-ordered spirit and a certain resemblance to the goodness of their Father, God, on the part of God's sons. It prays for everyone always and gives thanks for everything. It continually pours itself out before God in as many kinds of prayer or thanksgiving as its devout affection finds occasion in its needs or consolations, and also in sharing its neighbor's pains or joys. It is constantly absorbed in thanksgiving because to be in such a state is to be always in the joy of the Holy Spirit.[21]

---

17. William here draws from Eccles 1:18 as he frequently does in his writings (see e.g. Exp 29, 36, 122). It is a common theme in the writings of the Cistercian Fathers. Isaac of Stella develops it most deeply in the *Fourth Sermon for Sexagesima* (Cistercian Fathers Series 33). The observation that William is making here is a very good one, and one which undoubtedly he himself experienced: when God wishes to prove a soul, all the wise and judicious counsel which is given to him is of no help, in fact it only increases his anguish of soul. As William himself said in his *Second Meditation:* "For where shall I seek comfort, if desolation is your will for me?" (Med 2:2, CF 3:95).

18. Rom 7:18.   19. 1 Cor 13:8.

20. 1 Thess 5:17f.   21. 1 Thess 1:6.

XLV. 182. When it is a question of petitions prayer should be made devoutly and with faith but without obstinate persistence, since it is not we but our Father who is in heaven who knows what we need in these temporal things.[22]

183. But when it is a question of supplications then we should persist, yet with all humility and patience, because it is only in patience that they bear fruit.[23] Sometimes when grace is not quick in coming to the assistance the suppliant finds the heavens become bronze and the ground iron.[24] When the hardness of man's heart left to itself does not deserve to have its prayers heard the one in need thinks in his anxiety that he is being refused what in fact is only being withheld for a time. And when like the Canaanite woman he laments that he is being ignored and scorned[25] he imagines that his past sins are being imputed to him or made a matter of reproach like the uncleanness of a dog.[26]

184. Sometimes however, by dint of hard work, he obtains when he asks, he finds when he seeks, the door is opened to him when he knocks.[27] The toil of supplication is found worthy to obtain at length the consolations and sweetnesses of prayer.

XLVI. 185. Sometimes also the affections of pure prayer and that good sweetness of sentiment do not have to be looked for but take the initiative.[28] Without being asked or sought for, without any knocking, grace takes a man by surprise. It is as if one belonging to the servant class was welcomed to the table at which the sons of the family eat, when a soul that is still untrained and a beginner is taken up into the state of prayer which as a rule is given to the perfect, after they have earned it, as a reward for their sanctity.[29] When this happens it comes as a judgment making it impossible for the negligent soul to be unaware of what it is neglecting, or as

22. Mt 6:8. 23. Lk 8:15.
24. Deut 28:23; Cf. Exp 201, CF 6:161–162; Med 12:5, CF 3–169.
25. Mt 15:23. 26. Cf. Med 2:3, CF 3:96.
27. Mt 7:7f. 28. Cf. Exp 23, CF 6:17–18.
29. Cf. Exp 16, CF 6:13.

a stimulus to charity, kindling love in the soul for the grace that offers itself so freely.

186. In this matter, alas, very many are deceived. Fed as they are with the bread of children[30] they consider that they are in fact children now. They begin to fall back from the point from which they should be advancing and the result of the grace which came to them is that they play their conscience false, considering themselves to be of some importance whereas in fact they are nothing.[31] The Lord's gifts do not lead to any improvement in them but to a hardening of heart, so that they join those of which the Psalm says: "The Lord's enemies have lied to him and they will last to the end of the ages. Yet he fed them with rich grain and filled them with honey from the rock."[32] Servants as they are, they are fed by God the Father with the more choice food of grace, so that they may aspire to be children; but they turn God's grace to ill account and become his enemies. Making ill use even of the holy Scriptures in their sins or inordinate desires, when they go back to them after prayer they quote to themselves those words of Manoah's wife: "If the Lord had intended to kill us he would not have accepted the sacrifice from our hands."[33]

30. Mt 15:26.

31. Gal 6:3.

32. Ps 80:16f. We have here in this letter written in the evening of his life a theme which he had developed already in one of his first works, the treatise, *On the Nature and Dignity of Love*. There he also spoke of the grace of mystical union being granted to a beginner creating for him the same danger, one which all did not escape, and there he cites the same text from the Psalms, giving it the same interpretation. See NDL 11.

33. Judg 13:23.

BOOK TWO

INTRODUCTION

HOW LOVELY ARE YOUR TENTS, Lord of Hosts. In them the sparrow finds a home for itself and the turtledove a nest in which to lay its young."[1] The sparrow, I say, by nature an animal with evil inclinations, inconstant, unstable, a nuisance, loquacious and addicted to pleasure. And the turtledove, given to mourning, making its haunts in shady solitude, the pattern of simplicity and the model of chastity. The former finds for itself in your tents a peaceful and safe home, the latter a nest in which it can lay its young.

188. What are these but the young with their hot-blooded nature and fervent spirit, at an age at which falls come readily and curiosity is rampant; and those of riper years, in full possession of their manhood, with a spirit[2] that is serious, chaste, sober, wearied of outward things and as far as possible recollecting itself within itself?

189. Of these the former find in the tents of the Lord of Hosts, in the ordered life that is lived in cells, rest for themselves from all vices, encouragement in stability and a safe dwelling-place. While the latter find in the seclusion of the cell a hidden sanctuary for their conscience in which they can deposit and nourish the fruits of their holy affections and the understanding they have derived from spiritual contemplation. The sparrow all alone on the roof,[3] that is, in the heights of contemplation, takes pleasure in treading on the

---

1. Ps 83:2ff.   2. *Animus*—see above, n. 66, note 44.   3. Ps 101:8.

dwelling-place of its carnal life. The turtledove, at a lower level, is fecund and rejoices in the fruits of its humility.

190. The perfect, spiritual men, to whom the name of turtledove is given, in order to strengthen and consolidate their virtue, are always abasing themselves and stooping through the virtue of obedience and submission to the rank of beginners and so by descending beneath themselves they mount above themselves and by lowering themselves they make greater progress. They do not consider that the fruits of solitude, which are frequent and lofty flights of contemplation, entitle them to neglect the basic attitude of voluntary submission, the fellowship of the common life and the sweetness of fraternal charity.

II. 191. Therefore the spiritual man makes a spiritual use even of his body and wins from it a service that is not imposed by force as with the animal man, or obtained by repeated acts as in the case of the rational man, but as it were accorded by nature. While they receive an obedience deriving from necessity, he receives one that is prompted by charity. While they have virtues for which they have to work hard, he has virtues which have become second nature to him.

192. However, those sparrows of God, striving upwards toward the life of the perfect, not with the presumption that comes of pride but with the piety that is born of love, and in the poverty of their spirit, are not driven away as proud but welcomed as devout; and sometimes they are granted some experience of what properly belongs to the perfect. They always aspire to imitate the ascetic life[4] of those whose contemplative consolation they wish to make their own.

193. So moving forward with one spirit, although not with the same gait, spiritual men on the low ground and beginners in the heights make a like progress.

---

4. William has here *activam vitam*—the active life, understood in the sense in which it was taken in the Middle Ages, namely a life taken up with the exercise of the virtues, the moral life or as we have translated it, the ascetic life.

This is the holy intercourse which goes on between well regulated cells, their venerable pursuits, their busy leisure, their active repose, their ordered charity, to hold converse with one another in silence and to enjoy one another more while remaining apart from one another, to be an occasion of progress to one another, and although they do not see one another, to find matter for imitation each in the other, but in themselves only grounds for weeping.

194. "I," as the Prophet says, "am a man who see my own poverty."[5] When I reckon up the wealth of others I blush for myself and sigh because what I contemplate in another I would prefer to experience in myself. Surely it is the more tolerable of two evils not to see what you love than to see it and not to have it; however, it is not so with the good things of the Lord.[6] For to see the good things of the Lord is to love them and to love them is to have them. Therefore let us strive as far as possible to see, by seeing to understand, and by understanding to love, so that by loving we may possess. Lord, in this regard all my desire lies open before you and my groaning is not hidden from you.[7]

5. Lam 3:1.   6. Ps 26:13.   7. Ps 37:10.

THE RATIONAL MAN

TO PASS ON THEN from the animal state to the rational, so that from the rational we may pass on to the spiritual (and would that this transition in our treatment of the subject might be accompanied by a corresponding advance in reality), we must first of all know that Wisdom, as we read in the book that bears its name, "anticipates those who desire it and comes to meet them, joyfully revealing itself to them on the way."[1] Whether it be in the effort to advance or in meditation or in study "it reaches everywhere on account of its purity."[2] For God helps with his countenance[3] the man who looks upon him; the splendor of the Highest Good[4] moves and leads onward and attracts the man who contemplates it.

196. And when reason as it progresses mounts on high to become love, and grace comes down to meet the one who so loves and desires, it often happens that reason and love, which produce those two states, become one thing, and likewise wisdom and knowledge, which result from them. No longer can they be treated or thought of separately. They are now one thing, flowing from one activity and one faculty, both in the perception of understanding and in

---

1. Wis 6:14; Cf. NDL 28.   2. Wis 7:24.

3. Ps 44:6. The "face of God" is a biblical expression which is dear to William and found very frequently in his writings, e.g. Med 2:9; 3:2, 3; 6:2; 7:1ff; 8:1, 5; 9:5; 10:8; 11:1f; 12:5; MDL 9; Exp 35 (see note 17, CF 6:28-29).

4. William uses this same expression in the opening lines of his *Exposition on the Song of Songs*, n. 1, CF 6:3.

the joy of fruition. And so although each must be distinguished from the other, since the matter stands so, each must be thought and treated of with the other and in the other.

197. We have said above[5] that in spiritual progress the animal state is concerned with setting in order the body and the outward man and fitting them to the pursuit of virtue. Similarly the rational state must busy itself with the spirit,[6] either to bring it into being if it does not already exist, or to develop and regulate it if it does. First of all the question must be considered who or what is the spirit itself which the reason makes rational; and what the reason is which by making a mortal animal rational brings man to completion.

198. But first the spirit must be dealt with.

IV. The soul is something incorporeal, capable of reason, destined to impart life to the body. It is this which makes men animal, acquainted with the things of the flesh, cleaving to bodily sensation. But when it begins to be not only capable but also in possession of perfect reason, it immediately renounces the mark of the feminine and becomes spirit endowed with reason, fitted to rule the body,[7] spirit in possession of itself. For as long as it is soul it is quick to slip effeminately into what is of the flesh; but the spirit thinks only on what is virile and spiritual.

199. Man's spirit was created with an acute perception in the quest for good and with an active nature. In the womb of creative Wisdom it excelled every material object, shone brighter than all bodily light, and was of greater dignity because it was the image of its Creator and capable of reason. But it was implicated in the fault attached to its fleshly origin and made the slave of sin, taken captive by the law of sin which is in its members.[8]

5. See above, nn. 34, 71.
6. *Animum*, see above, n. 66, note 50. This masculine form, indicating that the soul now has become virile and manly, is usually translated in our text as "spirit" to distinguish it from the weaker and more feminine "soul"—*anima*.
7. St Augustine, *De quantitate animae*, 13 (PL 32:1048).
8. Rom 7:23. This seventh chapter of the Epistle to the Romans is evidently in the mind of William as he develops this passage.

H

200. Yet it did not wholly lose its power of choice, that is, the power of the reason to judge and to discern, although it lost its freedom to will and to act. For as a punishment for sin and as evidence of the natural dignity it had lost, the power of choice was left to it, although captive, as a sign. This even before the conversion and liberation of the will it can never wholly lose by any perversion of the will. Even when it abuses this power to choose evil instead of good, it is, as has been said, better and of greater dignity than any bodily creature, both in itself and in the womb of creative Wisdom.

201. Now the will is set free when it becomes charity: when the charity of God is poured out in our hearts by the Holy Spirit who is given to us.[9] And then reason is truly reason, that is a disposition of the mind ready to conform to the truth in all things. For when the will has been set free by liberating grace and the spirit begins to be moved by a reason that is free, then it becomes its own master, that is, it makes free use of itself; it becomes spirit and a good spirit. Spirit insofar as it imparts life well and brings its animal part to fulfillment by the addition of the ability to reason freely; good insofar as it now loves its good by which it becomes good and without which it could be neither good nor spirit.

202. Man endowed with spirit becomes good and rational, loving the Lord his God with his whole heart and his whole soul and all his mind and all his strength,[10] and, only in God, himself and his neighbor as himself.[11] He has the good spirit which fears God and keeps his commandments: this is the whole of man.[12]

203. Reason is defined or described by those whose business it is to define or describe as "a gaze of the spirit in which it looks upon truth not by means of the body but by itself; or the very contemplation of truth,"[13] or the truth itself contemplated, or rational life, or a rational service in which conformity is obtained with the truth that is contemplated.

---

9. Rom 5:5.   10. Mk 12:30.   11. Mk 12:31.

12. Eccles 12:13. This text is used by William with some frequency in his writings. See for example Exp 88; CG 8, 11.

13. St Augustine, *De immortalitate animae,* 6:10 (PL 32:1026a).

204. Reasoning is the process by which reason conducts its search, that is, the movement of its gaze through the things which are to be looked upon. Reasoning seeks, reason finds. This gaze cast upon an object is knowledge when a man sees the object, ignorance when he does not.[14]

205. Such is reason: both an instrument with which work is done and the work which is achieved. It tends always to exercise itself in what is useful and good; it makes progress through exercise but withers away through inactivity.

V. 206. Now there is no more worthy or more useful exercise for man endowed with reason than what involves the best of his endowments, that in which he excels other animals and the other parts of himself, his own mind[15] or spirit. But for the mind or spirit, to the rule of which the rest of man is subject, there is nothing more worthy to seek or sweeter to find or more useful to possess than the only thing which is superior to the mind—God alone.

207. Nor is he far from any of us, for it is in him that we live and move and have our being.[16] And it is not with the Lord our God as with this air, but in him we live through faith, we move and advance through hope, we have our being, that is, our fixed dwelling-place through love.

208. For it was by him and for him that the rational spirit was created, in order that its inclination might be toward him[17] and that he should be its good. It is from his goodness that it is good, it was created to his image and likeness,[18] in order that as long as its life here lasts it may approach as nearly and as truly as possible to him by resemblance from whom only dissimilarity brings about

14. St Augustine, *De quantitate animae*, 27:53 (PL 32:1065cd).

15. *Mens*—the superior part of the soul which is the place of encounter with God through divine illumination, the place of mystical experience: "If you are with me in your soul (*mens*), there I will repose with you; then I will feed you."—Exp 64, CF 6:51.

16. Acts 17:27f.   17. Song 7:10.   18. Gen 1:26.

distance.[19] Thus it would be holy here as he is holy[20] and in the next life happy as he is happy.

209. In a word all greatness and goodness for the spirit that is great and good consists in looking upon and wondering at and aspiring to what is above it, so that the devoted image hastens to cling to its exemplar.[21] For it is the image of God, and the fact that it is his image enables it to understand that it can and should cling to him whose image it is.

210. Therefore although upon earth its better part, its memory, understanding and love, rules the body which has been entrusted to it, it loves always to be engaged in the place from where it knows that it has received whatever it is, whatever it has.[22] There it hopes, to the extent man can so hope, if he does not fail to bring his life into line with his holy hope, to dwell forever and, with the full vision of God, to attain to a full resemblance to him.

211. There it is that the spirit's gaze is fixed, from there it depends, living with men more to impart to them God's life, to seek and obtain the things of God, than to live this mortal and human life.

212. It holds erect the body which it animates, raising it to its natural state, looking to the heaven that by nature and place and dignity transcends all places and all bodies.[23] In the same way, because of its spiritual nature, it loves to raise itself always to the things which are highest in the spiritual order, to God and the things of God—not by savoring proud thoughts but by loving devoutly and living soberly and justly and piously.[24] The higher the goal to which it aspires, the more vigorous must be the pursuits

19. St Augustine, *Enarr. in Psalmos*, 34:6; 94:2; 99:5.

20. 1 Jn 3:3.

21. The theology of man as the image of God is fundamental in the whole of the Cistercian school of spirituality. For an excellent study of this see A. Hallier, *The Monastic Theology of Aelred of Rievaulx* (Cistercian Studies Series 2) c. 1, pp. 3–24. William returns to this very frequently in his writings. See the Analytic Index in the different volumes of his *Works*.

22. 1 Cor 4:7.

23. Cf. NBS 9.

24. Tit 2:12.

in which it exercises itself. They must not only tint it but dye it thoroughly. Their effect on it must be to bring it to perfection.

VI. 213. Now although these pursuits may sometimes be helped by literature and make use of it, they are not merely literary, they are not concerned with mere trifles, with wrangling and gossip; they are spiritual, peaceful, humble, adapting themselves to humble men. They may be carried on exteriorly but their proper sphere is within a man's mind and spirit, where his renewal takes place[25] and he puts on the new self which is created in God's image, justified and sanctified through the truth.[26]

214. It is there that the spirit is fashioned, there that a good understanding is acquired by all those who seek for it,[27] there that in accord with the rule which the Apostle gives, "in all things we are taught to show ourselves as God's ministers, with great patience, in affliction, need, difficulty, hard work, vigils, in the prison of the cell, fasting, chastity, knowledge, forbearance, graciousness, relying on the Holy Spirit, on unfeigned charity, on the word of truth, on the power of God. To right and to left we are armed with justice, now honored, now slighted, now traduced, now flattered. They call us deceivers and we tell the truth; unknown and we are fully acknowledged; dying men, and see we live; punished, yes, but not doomed to die; sad men that rejoice continually; beggars that bring riches to many; disinherited and the world is ours,[28] in toil and weariness, in hunger and thirst, in cold and nakedness."[29]

215. These and the like are the holy pursuits, the exercises recommended by the Apostle in which the spirit which is alone with God examines and finds and corrects itself, cleansing itself from every defilement of flesh and spirit, completing the work of its sanctification in the fear of God.[30]

216. These are pursuits which love silence, long for tranquillity of heart in the midst of bodily toil, poverty of spirit and peace when in outward distress, a good conscience with complete purity

25. 2 Cor 4:16.   26. Eph 4:24.   27. Ps 110:10.
28. 2 Cor 6:4ff.   29. 2 Cor 11:27.   30. 2 Cor 7:1.

of both heart and body. It is these which make the spirit what it is, because they have the wherewithal. Whereas those empty studies, trifling, verbose, wrangling as they are, designed to feed curiosity and ambition, dissipate and corrupt the spirit even when it has been brought into being or is already perfect.

217. The others are pursuits which search into the roots rather than the flowers of the virtues. They aim rather at producing them than at making them shine, at gaining possession of them rather than at knowing about them.

VII. 218. With regard to vices such men are more afraid of the evil desires which arise in themselves than of assaults coming from other people. They fear infection more than violence. For just as sometimes by dint of much hard work and persevering effort the virtues come to influence a man's affections and give him a right outlook, so the vices avail themselves of the slightest relaxation or disorder to insinuate themselves into his character and become as it were natural.

219. But no vice is natural to man, whereas virtue is.[31] None the less the force of habit deriving from a corrupt will or a deep-seated carelessness tends to make a host of vices become as if natural to the conscience which has been neglected. As medical men say, habit is second nature.

220. Yet every bad spirit can be softened before it grows hard in evil; and even after it has become hardened it need not be despaired of. For the curse pronounced upon Adam[32] means that the earth which we cultivate and the ground which is our heart or body produce harmful or useless growth freely in all directions, but what is useful and necessary only with hard work.

221. However, since virtue is a product of nature, when eventually it comes into the spirit it comes, not indeed without hard work, yet as to its own proper place, and there it settles down to stay. Nature is well pleased with it, for it knows no greater reward than to be aware of itself in God.

---

31. Cf. Exp 125, CF 6:101.   32. Gen 3:17ff.

222. However, vice although it is considered to be nothing other than the privation of virtue can assume such enormous proportions as to be felt crushing and overwhelming. Its vileness can be such that it defiles and infects. It can cling with so pertinacious a force of habit that nature is scarcely able to shake it off.

223. For it is in vain that every rivulet of vice is dried up if the source is not stopped up. For example, a will that has slackened leads to levity of mind, from which there proceed instability of disposition, inconstancy in behavior, empty-headed joy that often reaches the point of carnal indulgence and groundless sorrow that sometimes causes even bodily sickness; and many other evils arise from the vice of levity and lead to neglect or abandonment of vocation.

So also a will that has grown proud through habit often inflates the spirit with pride while the heart is dried up. From such a state of affairs there proceed vain glory, trust in oneself, neglect of God, boasting, disobedience, scorn, presumption and the other diseases of the spirit which usually arise from conceit and the habit of pride.

224. In this way every kind of vice derives its origin from some disorder of the will or from the force of bad habit. The more attractive to the mind it is and the more firmly rooted, the more tenaciously it clings and the more vigorous are the remedies it calls for and the more painstaking the care it needs.

225. For diseases of this sort, vices, pursue the solitary into the furthest recesses of his solitude. And just as solid virtue that is firmly established in the spirit does not abandon the man who possesses it however many people there may be around him, so the vice of bad habit leaves the man over whom it has asserted its mastery no freedom in any solitude. For unless the habit be rooted out by persevering effort and prudent toil, it may be attenuated but it can hardly be overcome. However carefully the spirit may set itself in order, the habit clings; in whatever degree of solitude it dwells, the habit precludes solitude or silence in the heart.

226. The stronger the bent of the habit, and of the will, the more powerfully is felt the rebellion of what may be termed not so much spiritual malice as a swarm of pests of all sorts or a heavy

tumor weighing down the body that must be cast out as it were with manual force.

VIII.   227. But let us return to the praise of virtue. What is virtue? It is the daughter of reason, but still more of grace. It is a certain force issuing from nature but it derives from grace the fact that it is virtue.[33] The approving judgment of reason makes it a force, but the desire of an enlightened will makes it virtue. For virtue is a willing assent to good;[34] virtue is a certain balance of life, conforming to reason in all things. Virtue is the use of free will according to the judgment of reason. Virtue is a certain humility, a certain patience. It embraces obedience, prudence, temperance, fortitude, justice and very many other qualities, in each of which virtue is nothing other than, as has been said, the use of free will in accordance with the judgment of reason.

228. For a will that is good is the source of all good in the soul and the mother of all the virtues. Contrariwise an evil will gives rise to all evils and vices. Therefore one who keeps guard over his soul should be very anxious in his watch over his will, so that he may understand and discern wisely what is or ought to be the universal object of volition, the love of God, and what is a subordinate object, for example, love of vocation.

229. For every indiscretion to be safe in the former there must always be in the latter a vigilant and prudent discretion, according to the rules of obedience.

230. In the love of God all reason and all discretion amount to this: as he in his love for us went to the limit of love[35] so, if possible, we should love him without any limit, just as that man is happy whose desire to keep his commandments is without bounds.[36]

---

33. In eliciting an act of virtue there is a certain force at work which comes from nature but for the act to be truly virtuous it is necessary that grace inform it to its very depths and give it its finality. For this reason for William the virtues of the pagans were not in truth true virtues. See Exp 105; CG 12.

34. Cf. Med 5:7, CF 3:121.

35. Jn 13:1.

36. Ps 111:1.

IX. 231. But although the gift of self which is prompted by love should be without any limit or bound, external activity should be kept within fixed limits and governed by rule. In this regard, to prevent excesses on the part of the will, truth must always be present keeping guard by means of obedience.

232. For nothing is of greater advantage to the man who is making progress on his way to God than will and truth. These are the two which, as our Lord says: "If they agree in asking for anything, whatever it may be, they will obtain it from their Father, God."[37]

233. If these two things are in perfect accord, combining to form one principle, they contain in themselves all the plenitude of the virtues without the interference of any vice. They are capable of anything even in a man who has no strength; they are endowed with everything and possess everything in the man who has no possessions; they give, lend, contribute, make themselves useful in the man who is living quietly in retirement. There are glory and wealth in the soul of that blessed man,[38] issuing from the fruits of his good will. Externally he is protected not only on one side, as with the shields of this world, but on all sides by the shield of God's truth.[39] For interiorly he is made always cheerful and pleasant by good will, while in outward activity truth keeps him grave and serious, safe and assured. Therefore that man rises above the things of men and is always tranquil, as men tell of the air above the moon.[40]

X. 234. The will is a natural appetite of the soul with various objects: now God and the interior life, now the body and external things relating to the body.

37. Mt 18:19.

38. Ps 111:3. Cf. Exp 67, 118, CF 6:54, 95.

39. Ps 90:5.

40. An idea taken from the Stoics. See Seneca, *Letters to Lucilius,* 59:16; trans. R. M. Gummere, *The Epistles of Seneca,* vol. 1 (Cambridge: Harvard, 1934), p. 421. Cf. Exp 203, CF 6:163.

235. When the will mounts on high, like fire going up to its proper place,[41] that is to say when it unites with truth and tends to higher things, it is "love." When it is fed with the milk of grace in order to make progress it is "dilection"; when it lays hold of its object and keeps it in its grasp and has enjoyment of it, it is "charity," it is unity of spirit, it is God.[42] For God is charity.[43] But in these matters a man is only beginning when he arrives at the end,[44] for they do not admit of full perfection in this life.

236. When the will turns aside to the things of the flesh, it is carnal concupiscence. When it is governed by worldly curiosity, it is concupiscence of the eyes. When it makes glory or honor its ambition, it is the pride of life.[45]

237. Yet as long as in such things it serves the advantage or the necessities of nature, it is nature or natural appetite. When, however, it abandons itself to superfluous or harmful objects, it is a vice of nature or a vicious will. You will find the proof of this in yourself, in the first movement of desire. When it is a question of bodily necessities and the will goes no further than the first desire, it is the soul's natural appetite. But when its desires extend ever further and further, it betrays itself. It is no longer will but a vice of the will, avarice or covetousness or something of that sort. For the will is soon satisfied in such matters, while its vices never have enough.[46]

XI. 238. In spiritual things and matters relating to God the will is praiseworthy when it takes as its object something that is within its reach. When it wills something outside or exceeding its possibilities it must be governed and checked. When it does not will what is within its reach it must be aroused and stimulated. For often if it is not kept in check it breaks away and rushes headlong to disaster. Often if it is not stirred up it sleeps and delays, forgets its destination and easily turns aside, letting itself be caught in the shackles of any pleasure that may offer itself.

41. Cf. NDL 1.
42. For a similar enumeration of the types of names of love, see Exp 6, CF. 6:8.
43. 1 Jn 4:16.   44. Sir 18:6.   45. 1 Jn 2:16.   46. Cf. NDL 4f.

239. Therefore, as is usually the case with the body too (for a man's body is seen better by another than by himself), in such matters the eye of someone else often has a clearer view of us than our own. Someone else, someone whose will is not a prey to the same fervor, is often a better judge of our acts than we are. For often either through negligence or through self-love we have a mistaken idea of ourselves.

240. Therefore obedience is a trusty guardian of the will, whether it be obedience to a command or to advice, whether it involve subordination or be prompted by charity alone. For, as the Apostle Peter says,[47] those who practice obedience often cleanse their hearts more effectively and more smoothly by submitting to their equals or even to their inferiors in the obedience of charity than by subjection to their superiors in the obedience of necessity. In the former case it is charity alone that orders or advises and obeys, while in the latter there is the fear of punishment or the threat of an imperious authority or constraining necessity. In the former case greater glory is owing to him who obeys, while in the latter disobedience incurs greater punishment.

241. It is clear to all therefore how necessary it is for the man whose heart is raised on high that his will should have due custody, to govern, regulate and order his exterior, but even more for the sake of his interior. For when a soul often thinks of itself or of God the will is the starting point of all its thoughts and it is by this starting point that the whole character of his thinking is determined.

XII.   242. Three things go to make up thought: will, memory and intellect. The will impels the memory to bring forth the matter, it impels the intellect to give shape to what is brought forth. It applies the intellect to the memory so that the concept may be formed from it. To the intellect it applies the power of thought so that the concept may spring from it. It is because the will impels these two principles into one and joins them by its effortless behest that

47. 1 Pet 1:22.

cogitatio (thought) seems to receive its name from *cogendo* (impelling).[48]

243. This is the origin of all thoughts, some good and holy and worthy of God, others evil and perverse, which separate from God, others without sense, idle and empty, from which God removes himself. That is why it is said: "Evil thoughts separate from God,"[49] and "The Holy Spirit keeps far away from thoughts which are without sense."[50]

244. In regard to these words it should be observed that without some sense it is impossible to think at all and no thought whatever is without some sense. But there is one sense that derives from the natural force of reason and another that comes from the higher reaches of the mind. It is the same power of understanding which, to whatever object it be applied, whether for good or for evil, exercises its natural vigor, but it differs according as it is left to itself or enlightened by grace.

245. In the former case it yields itself to the affairs of the world, both serious and trifling. In the latter case it gives its attention only to things that are worthy of itself and resemble it. In the former case it often acts as left to itself, infected with vice through the power of the reason and the fault of the corrupted will, devising perverse thoughts by which it freely separates itself, from God, their author. But in the latter case it is always enlightened and dedicated to virtue; its activity is characterized by piety which unites it in its thoughts with God.[51]

XIII. 246. The thoughts without any sense mentioned above in the second place[52] are those empty and idle thoughts which are not brought under either kind of understanding, for lack of serious

---

48. St Augustine, *De Trinitate*, 11:3, 6; trans. S. McKenna, *The Trinity* (Washington: Catholic University, 1963), p. 322. The same derivation appears also in the *Confessions*, 10:11; trans. Pilkington, p. 156.

49. Wis 1:3.   50. Wis 1:5.

51. At the beginning of this letter William defined piety in this sense. See above, n. 9.

52. See above, n. 243.

attention on the part of their author. They do not lead to instant destruction but bring about a slow and gradual corruption. They take up the time, distract the attention from necessary business and poison the mind. They are not so much thoughts as ghosts of thoughts arising from true or imaginary recollections of thoughts, or these recollections themselves welling up uncalled for and in many shapes from the memory.

247. The will would seem to be passive rather than active where they are concerned, since they do not involve any deliberation on the part of the mind. What bursts forth from the memory of its own accord presents itself, to be shaped into a concept, to an intellect which pays no attention to it. Whatever it is that is taking place seems to be happening rather in a dream than as a result of any effort on the part of the subject. He may have no intention of driving the Holy Spirit away from himself, but that is what happens through his culpable negligence. The Spirit which loves discipline rightly removes to a distance from undisciplined thoughts.

248. Such thoughts may arise from a certain hidden power of the reason but they do not come from the reason itself and the intellect is drawn into them without any consent on the part of the subject.[53]

But when serious thought is properly devoted to serious matters, the will, acting on the free deliberation of the reason, calls forth from the memory whatever is needed, applies the intellect to the memory to form a concept, and when it is formed, such as it may be, the intellect submits it to the examination of the subject: so it is that the process of thought is completed.[54]

53. William speaks pointedly of this weakness of distractions and the suffering that comes from them as well as the final victory that can be hoped for in his *Exposition on the Song of Songs* (nn. 61, 144, 178).

54. As Dom Déchanet indicates: "This digression on thinking and thoughts (242–248) has for its purpose to show us that the perfection of the rational man (which coincides with the birth of the spiritual man—see n. 44) consists in an ever greater effort of the will to orient the activity of the thinker toward God and the things of God."—*Lettre d'Or,* p. 180, note 261.

THE SPIRITUAL MAN

THE PERFECTION OF MAN IN THIS LIFE

WHEN THE OBJECT OF THOUGHT is God and the things which relate to God and the will reaches the stage at which it becomes love, the Holy Spirit, the Spirit of life, at once infuses himself by way of love and gives life to everything, lending his assistance in prayer, in meditation or in study to man's weakness. Immediately the memory becomes wisdom and tastes with relish the good things of the Lord, while the thoughts to which they give rise are brought to the intellect to be formed into affections. The understanding of the one thinking becomes the contemplation of one loving and it shapes it into certain experiences of spiritual or divine sweetness which it brings before the gaze of the spirit so that the spirit rejoices in them.

250. And then, insofar as it is possible for man, worthy thoughts are entertained of God, if indeed the word "thought" (*cogitatio*) is correct where there is no impelling principle (*cogit*) nor anything impelled (*cogitur*),[1] but only awareness of God's abundant sweetness leading to exultation,[2] jubilation and a true experience of the Lord in goodness on the part of the man who has sought him in this simplicity of heart.[3]

1. See above, n. 242, note 48.
2. Ps 144:7.
3. Wis 1:1. A key text in the mystical doctrine of William of St Thierry We have in these first three paragraphs of his treatment of the Spiritual Man a summary of his teaching concerning the contemplative experience of God.

251. But this way of thinking about God does not lie at the disposal of the thinker. It is a gift of grace, bestowed by the Holy Spirit who breathes where he chooses, when he chooses,[4] how he chooses and upon whom he chooses. Man's part is continually to prepare his heart by ridding his will of foreign attachments, his reason or intellect of anxieties, his memory of idle or absorbing, sometimes even of necessary business, so that in the Lord's good time and when he sees fit, at the sound of the Holy Spirit's breathing the elements which constitute thought may be free at once to come together and do their work, each contributing its share to the outcome of joy for the soul. The will displays pure affection for the joy which the Lord gives, the memory yields faithful material, the intellect affords the sweetness of experience.

XV. 252. A will that is neglected gives rise to thoughts that are idle and unworthy of God; a will that is corrupted yields thoughts that are perverse and alienated from God; a rightly ordered will leads to thoughts that are necessary for the living of this life; a dutiful will engenders thoughts which are rich in the fruits of the Spirit and bring enjoyment of God. "Now the fruits of the Spirit," the Apostle tells us, "are charity, joy, peace, patience, forbearance, goodness, kindness, meekness, faith, modesty, chastity, continence."[5]

253. In every kind of thought all that occurs to the mind conforms to the intention of the will through the intervention of God's mercy and judgment, so that the just man is made still more just and the man who is defiled becomes still more defiled.[6]

254. Therefore the man who desires to love the Lord or already loves him should always question his spirit and examine his conscience as to the object and motive of his basic desire; ask, too, what else the spirit wills or hates and what inordinate desires the flesh entertains in opposition to it.[7]

255. For the desires which make their way in as if from outside and then disappear and those which brush against the soul in

4. Jn 3:8.   5. Gal 5:22f.   6. Gal 22:11.   7. Gal 5:17.

passing, so that at one moment it feels desire and at the next moment feels none, are not to be counted among the objects of volition but only among idle thoughts. They may even go as far as to cause the mind some pleasure, but none the less it quickly shakes itself free of them if it is its own master.[8]

256. As to the basic desire, first of all the object of desire should be considered, then the extent to which it is desired and the way in which it is desired. If a man's basic desire is for God he should examine how much and in what way he desires God, whether to the point of despising self and everything which either exists or can exist, and this not only in accordance with the reason's judgment but also following the mind's inclination, so that the will is now something more than will: love, dilection, charity and unity of spirit.[9]

257. For such is the way in which God is to be loved. "Love" is a strong inclination of the will toward God, "dilection" is a clinging to him or a union with him; "charity" is the enjoyment of him.[10] But "unity of spirit" with God for the man who has his heart raised on high is the term of the will's progress toward God. No longer does it merely desire what God desires, not only does it love him, but it is perfect in its love, so that it can will only what God wills.[11]

258. Now to will what God wills is already to be like God, to be able to will only what God wills is already to be what God is; for him to will and to be are the same thing. Therefore it is well said that we shall see him fully as he is when we are like him,[12] that is when we are what he is. For those who have been enabled to become sons of God[13] have been enabled to become not indeed God, but what God is: holy, and in the future, fully happy as God is. And the source of their present holiness and their future happiness is none other than God himself who is at once their holiness and their happiness.

8. See above, n. 248, note 53.   9. See above, n. 235.
10. Cf. above, n. 49.   11. Cf. below, nn. 262f.
12. 1 Jn 3:2. Note that William has inverted the saying of the Apostle.
13. Jn 1:12.

XVI. 259. Resemblance to God is the whole of man's perfection. To refuse to be perfect is to be at fault. Therefore the will must always be fostered with this perfection in view and love made ready. The will must be prevented from dissipating itself on foreign objects, love preserved from defilement. For to this end alone were we created and do we live, to be like God; for we were created in his image.[14]

260. There is however a likeness to God which is lost only with life itself, left to every man by the Creator of all men as evidence of a better and more sublime likeness that has been lost. It is possessed regardless of acceptance or refusal, alike by the man who is capable of conceiving it and by the man who is so stupid that he cannot conceive it. It consists in the fact that, as God is everywhere, and is present with the whole of his being in his creation, so every living soul is in like manner present in its body.[15] And as God is never unlike himself, and without any unlikeness carries out dissimilar operations in his creation, so, although man's soul vivifies the whole of the body with one and the same life, in the bodily senses and in the thoughts of the heart without any unlikeness it is constantly carrying out dissimilar operations. As far as merit is concerned this likeness to God in man is of no importance with God, since it derives from nature, not from will or effort.

261. But there is another likeness, one closer to God, inasmuch as it is freely willed. It consists in the virtues and inspires the soul as it were to imitate the greatness of Supreme Good by the greatness of its virtue and his unchangeable eternity by its unwearying perseverance in good.

262. In addition to this there is yet another likeness, of which something has been said already.[16] It is so close in its resemblance that it is styled not merely a likeness but unity of spirit. It makes man one with God, one spirit, not only with the unity which comes of willing the same thing but with a greater fullness of virtue, as has been said: the inability to will anything else.

263. It is called unity of spirit not only because the Holy Spirit

14. Gen 1:26.   15. Cf. NBS 3, 12.   16. See above, nn. 257f.

I

brings it about or inclines a man's spirit to it, but because it is the Holy Spirit himself, the God who is Charity. He who is the Love of Father and Son, their Unity, Sweetness, Good, Kiss, Embrace and whatever else they can have in common in that supreme unity of truth and truth of unity, becomes for man in regard to God in the manner appropriate to him what he is for the Son in regard to the Father or for the Father in regard to the Son through unity of substance. The soul in its happiness finds itself standing midway in the Embrace and the Kiss of Father and Son. In a manner which exceeds description and thought, the man of God is found worthy to become not God but what God is, that is to say man becomes through grace what God is by nature.[17]

XVII. 264. That is why in his list of spiritual exercises the Apostle prudently inserted the Holy Spirit. He says: "In chastity, in knowledge, in forbearance, in graciousness, in the Holy Spirit, in unfeigned charity, in the word of truth, in the power of God."[18] See how he put the Holy Spirit in the midst of the good virtues, like the heart in the middle of the body, doing and ordering everything, imparting life to everything.

265. For he is the almighty Artificer who creates man's good will in regard to God, inclines God to be merciful to man, shapes man's desire, gives strength, ensures the prosperity of undertakings, conducts all things powerfully and disposes everything sweetly.[19]

266. He it is who gives life to man's spirit and holds it together, just as it gives life to its body and holds it together. Men may teach how to seek God and angels how to adore him, but he alone teaches how to find him, possess him and enjoy him. He himself is the anxious quest of the man who truly seeks, he is the devotion of the man who adores in spirit and truth, he is the wisdom of the man who finds, the love of him who possesses, the gladness of him who enjoys.

17. To get a full understanding of the sublime doctrine which William here presents, see Exp 95; MF 31; Med 6:7f.; see also the excellent note in this place in Déchanet, *op. cit.,* p. 182, note 277.

18. 2 Cor 6:6f.   19. Wis 8:1.

267. Yet whatever he bestows here on his faithful of the vision and the knowledge of God is but as in a mirror and a riddle,[20] as far removed from the vision and the knowledge that is to be in the future as faith is from truth or time from eternity. This is true even when what we read in the book of Job happens: "He hides the light in his hands and commands it to mount on high, then he tells his beloved that it belongs to him and that he can ascend to it."[21]

XVIII. 268. For the man who is chosen and loved by God is sometimes shown a certain light of God's countenance, just as light that is enclosed in a man's hands appears and is hidden at the will of him who holds it. This is in order that what he is allowed to glimpse for a passing moment may set the soul on fire with longing for full possession of eternal light, the inheritance of full vision of God.

269. To make him realize to some extent what he lacks,[22] grace sometimes as if in passing touches the affections of the lover and takes him out of himself, drawing him into the light of true reality, out of the tumult of affairs into the joys of silence, and to the slight extent of which he is capable, showing him for a moment, for an instant, ultimate reality as it is in itself.[23] Sometimes it even transforms the man into a resemblance of ultimate reality, granting him to be, to the slight extent of which he is capable, such as it is.

270. Then when he has learned the difference between the clean and the unclean[24] he is restored to himself and sent back to cleanse his heart for vision, to fit his spirit for likeness, so that if at some future date he should again be admitted to it he may be the more pure for seeing and able to remain for a longer time in the enjoyment of it.

271. For the limits of human imperfection are never better realized than in the light of God's countenance,[25] in the mirror which is the vision of God. Then in the light of true reality man sees more and more what he lacks and continually corrects by means of

---

20. I Cor 13:12.   21. Job 36:32f. (Septuagint). Cf. MF 31.
22. Ps 38:5.   23. I Jn 3:2.   24. Ezek 44:23.   25. Ps 4:7.

likeness whatever sins he has committed through unlikeness, drawing near by means of likeness to him from whom he has been separated by unlikeness. And so clearer vision is always accompanied by a clearer likeness.

272. It is impossible indeed for the supreme Good to be seen and not loved, or not to be loved to the full extent to which vision of it has been granted. So eventually love arrives at some likeness of that love which made God like to man by accepting the humiliation of our human lot in order that man might be made like to God by receiving the glorification of communion in the divine life. Then indeed it is sweet for man to be abased together with supreme Majesty, to become poor together with the Son of God,[26] to be conformed to divine Wisdom, to make his own the mind which is in Christ Jesus our Lord.[27]

XIX. 273. For here there is wisdom with devotion, love with fear, exultation with trembling,[28] when God is thought of and understood as brought down unto death, the death of the Cross,[29] to the end that man might be exalted to the likeness of the godhead. From here there flows the rushing stream that gladdens God's city,[30] the remembrance of his abounding sweetness[31] in the understanding and consideration of the benefits he has conferred on us.

274. In this regard man is easily led to love God by thinking about or contemplating what is worthy of love in him, which of itself shines upon the affections of the contemplative: his power and strength and glory and majesty and goodness and beatitude. But what especially carries man away in his spiritual love into the object of his love is that God in himself is whatever there is lovable in him; he is in the whole of himself what he is, if one can speak of a whole where there is no part.

275. In his love of this good the devout man who has been so

26. This was part of the expressed ideal of the Cistercian Founders: "To be poor with the poor of Christ."—*Exordium Parvum*, 15.

27. Phil 2:5.   28. Ps 2:11.   29. Phil 2:8.

30. Ps 45:5.   31. Ps 144:7.

affected centers himself upon it in such a way as not to be distracted from it until he becomes one or one spirit with him. Once arrived at this point he is separated and kept at a distance only by the veil of this mortality from the Holy of Holies and from that supreme beatitude of highest heaven. Yet since he already enjoys it in his soul through his faith and hope in him whom he loves, he is able to bear what is left of this life also with a more ready patience.

XX. 276. This is the goal for which the solitary strives, this is the end he has in view, this is his reward, the rest that comes after his labors, the consolation for his pains; and this is the perfection and the true wisdom of man. It embraces within itself and contains all the virtues, and they are not borrowed from another source but as it were naturally implanted in it, so that it resembles God who is himself whatever he is. Just as God is what he is, so the disposition of the good will in regard to the good of virtue is so firmly established in the good mind[32] and impressed on it that in its ardent clinging to unchangeable Good it seems utterly unable to change from what it is.

277. For when that "taking up by the Lord, the Holy One of Israel, our King,"[33] befalls the man of God, the wise and devout soul, with grace to enlighten and assist it, in the contemplation of supreme Good gazes also upon the laws of unchangeable Truth to the extent that it is found worthy to attain to them by means of the understanding that comes of love. From this it forms for itself a way of life which is heavenly and a model of holiness.

For it gazes upon supreme Truth and everything which derives truth from it, upon supreme Good and everything which derives goodness from it, upon supreme Eternity and everything which derives from it. It models itself upon that Truth, that Charity and that Eternity while directing its life here below. It does not fly above those eternal realities in its judgment but gazes up at them in desire or clings to them by love, while it accepts the realities of this created world to adapt and conform itself to them, not without using its

32. Cf. Exp 19, CF 6:14.   33. Ps 88:19.

judgment to discriminate, its power of reasoning to examine and its mind to appreciate.

278. This process gives rise to holy virtues, the image of God is formed anew in man, and that divine life is set in order from which the Apostle complains that certain men have become estranged.[34] Virtue also takes on its true vigor, those two elements which constitute the perfection of the contemplative and the active life,[35] concerning which, according to the ancient translators, we read in Job: "Behold piety is wisdom, while to abstain from evil is knowledge."[36]

279. For wisdom is indeed piety, that is, the worship of God, the love by which we yearn to see him and, seeing him in a mirror obscurely,[37] believe and hope in him and advance even to see him as he reveals himself.

280. But to abstain from evil is the knowledge of temporal matters with which our life here below is concerned. In their regard we abstain from evil to the extent to which we pursue good.

XXI. 281. This knowledge, this abstinence involve in the first place the practice of all the virtues and then the study of all the arts which govern this life which we are living. The former of these,

34. Eph 4:18.

35. "Active life" is here to be understood in the patristic sense. that is, life concerned with asceticism and the practice of the virtues.

36. Job 28:28 (Septuagint). In this and the following paragraph William is undoubtedly dependent on Augustine (*De Trinitate*, 12:14; PL 42:1010A, CC 50:375:17–29; trans. S. McKenna, *The Trinity,* Fathers of the Church, vol. 45 [Washington: Catholic U Press, 1963] pp. 363f). This gives us a key to a phrase which William frequently attributes to Job (e.g., above, n. 26; Exp 39, 172; NDL 7) but which is not actually found in him, not even in the Septuagint. The Septuagint has what William says here: "piety is wisdom," rather than his other expression: "piety is the worship of God." This he goes on to bring in here in the next sentence, and this he draws from Augustine: "I find it written in the book of Job, where that same holy man is speaking: 'Behold, piety is wisdom. . . .' In this same distinction it is to be understood that wisdom pertains to contemplation, science to action. For by piety in this passage he meant the worship of God. . . ." I am grateful to Father Stanley Cegler SDB for pointing this out to me.

37. 1 Cor 13:12.

the practice of the virtues, seems to be concerned rather with higher things, as displaying the power of higher wisdom and exhaling its fragrance. The latter, which is concerned with bodily exercises, sinks miserably into the vanity of this world if it is not held back by the bonds of religious faith.

282. In regard to these, since knowledge is something which is grasped either by the reason or by the bodily senses and committed to the memory, upon mature consideration it appears that only what is perceived by the senses can properly speaking be attributed to knowledge. As for what the reason conceives of itself in such matters, it is already on the borderland between knowledge and wisdom.

283. For whatever is learned from another source, that is, through the bodily senses, is taken into the mind as something foreign, coming from without. But what enters the mind of its own accord, whether through the mere exercise of the reason or by a natural understanding of the unchangeable laws of unchangeable Truth, which sometimes enables the most wicked of men to form a judgment that is wholly right, this is in the reason in such a way as to be identified with the reason. It is not given to it by any process of teaching, so as to be knowledge, but rather is understood to be present naturally either when someone else points this out or when the reason adverts to it itself.

284. The outstanding example of this is when the knowledge of God is revealed to a man,[38] even a godless man, by a natural manifestation on God's part. Then there is the case of a natural inclination to the virtues, of which a pagan poet was able to say that "The good hate sin for love of virtue."[39] Again there are all the distinctions made among the objects of the reason by the processes of investigation and reasoning.

285. The lowest type of knowledge and that which tends downwards is animal experience of sensible objects coming in

38. Rom 1:19. Cf. MDL 41; MF 24, 27.

39. Horace, *Letters,* 1:16; trans. E. Wickham, *Horace for English Readers* (London: Oxford University Press, 1930), p. 300. William employs this same citation in Exp 105 and CG 12.

through the five bodily senses. This is especially so when the lust of the flesh or of the eyes or the pride of this life[40] are involved.

XXII. 286. And so when reason in conformity with wisdom forms a conscience and draws up a rule of life, in the lower kinds of knowledge it avails itself of nature's services and resources, in reasonings and the things of the reason it follows the rule it has laid down, in the acquisition of virtues it obeys its conscience. Thus making progress by means of lower things, finding assistance in higher things, continuing on its way toward what is right it brings into play the judgment of reason, the assent of the will, the inclination of the mind and external activity and so hastens to arrive at liberty and unity of spirit, in order that, as has already been said often, the man of faith may become one spirit with God.[41]

287. Now this is the life of God of which we spoke a little while before,[42] not so much an advance in reason as an attachment of the affections to perfection in wisdom. For the fact that a man relishes these things makes him wise[43] and it is because he has become one spirit with God that he is spiritual. And this is the perfection of man in this life.

XXIII. 288. Hitherto solitary or alone, now he becomes one and his bodily solitude is changed into unity of spirit. Our Lord's prayer for his disciples, summing up the whole of perfection, is fulfilled in him: "Father, my will is that as I and you are one, so they too may be one in us."[44]

289. For insofar as this unity of man with God or likeness to God draws near to God, it brings into conformity with itself what is inferior to it, and with that what is lower still; so that the spirit, the soul and the body are duly set in order and established in their

---

40. 1 Jn 2:16.   41. 1 Cor 6:17. See above, nn. 262, 263, 275.
42. Above, n. 276f.

43. The play on words here is lost in the translation: *quia sapiunt sapienti, sapiens est.*

44. Jn 17:21.

proper places, rightly appreciated and even thought about in accordance with their several characteristics. So man begins to know himself perfectly, advance through self-knowledge and ascend to the knowledge of God.[45]

290. When the man who is making progress first begins to fix his desire and aspirations on this object he must be on his guard as he ponders on that likeness against the error of unlikeness, that is to say when he compares spiritual things with spiritual and divine things with divine, he must not think of them otherwise than they are in reality.[46]

291. Therefore when the spirit thinks of its likeness to God let it first mold its thought so as wholly to avoid conceiving of itself in terms of a body. Where God is concerned not only must it avoid thinking of him as of a body, as if he were in a place, but also as if he could be represented as a spirit and so changeable. For spiritual things are as different from corporeal things both in quality and in nature as they are remote from all confinement to place. The divine nature, however, transcends both corporeal and spiritual things to the same extent that it is free from all restrictions of time and place and knows nothing of change, remaining changeless and eternal in the beatitude of its own unchangeableness and eternity.

292. Just as the spirit has perception of corporeal things through the bodily senses, so it knows things pertaining to the reason or the spirit only through itself. But the things of God[47] it can seek or expect to understand only by God's gift. Indeed it is lawful and possible for man possessed of reason to think and enquire sometimes of some things which concern God, such as the sweetness of his goodness, the power of his strength and other like matters. But what he is in himself, his essence, can only be grasped by thought at all insofar as the perception of enlightened love reaches out to it.

---

45. Knowledge of self as an essential step toward knowledge of God is a common patristic theme which William develops at greater length in the *Exposition on the Song of Songs*, n. 62ff. See a parallel treatment in Bernard of Clairvaux, *On the Song of Songs*, Sermon Thirty-seven (Cistercian Fathers Series 7).

46. Cf. with the warning in MF 31ff.   47. Mt 22:21.

XXIV. 293. Yet God is to be attained by faith and, to the extent that the Holy Spirit helps our weakness,[48] by thought as Eternal Life living and bestowing life; the Unchangeable and immutably making all changeable things; the Intelligent and creating all understanding and every intellectual being; Wisdom that is the source of all wisdom; fixed Truth that stands fast without any swerving, the Source of all truth and containing from eternity the principles of all things that exist in time.

294. His life itself is his essence, his very nature. He is his own life by which he lives, and it is divinity, eternity, greatness, goodness and strength existing and subsisting in itself, transcending all place in the power of a nature not bounded by place, by its eternity rising above all time that can be conceived by reason or imagination. It exists in a manner that is far more true and excellent than can be grasped by any kind of perception. Yet humble and enlightened love attains to a more certain perception of it than any effort of the reason to grasp it by thought, and it is always better than it is thought to be. Yet it is better thought than spoken of.[49]

295. It is the supreme Essence, from which all being comes forth. It is the supreme Substance, not confined within the predicaments we formulate but the subsistent causal Principle of all things.[50] In it our being does not die, our understanding makes no mistake, our love meets with no offence. It is always sought in order that it may be found with greater pleasure and is found with utmost pleasure in order that it may be sought the more diligently.[51]

XXV. 296. Since this ineffable reality can be seen only in an ineffable way, the man who would see it must cleanse his heart, for it cannot be seen or apprehended by means of any bodily likeness in sleep, any bodily form in waking hours, any investigation of the mind, but only by humble love from a clean heart.[52]

48. Rom 8:26.
49. St Augustine, *De Trinitate,* 7:4; trans. McKenna, p. 229.
50. Cf. MF 27.
51. St Augustine, *De Trinitate,* 15:2; trans. McKenna, p. 452.
52. Mt 5:8.

297. For this is the face of God which no one can see and live in the world.[53] This is the Beauty for the contemplation of which everyone sighs who would love the Lord his God with his whole heart and his whole soul and his whole mind and his whole strength.[54] Neither does he cease to arouse his neighbor to the same if he loves him as himself.[55]

298. When eventually he is admitted to this vision he sees without any doubt in the light of truth the grace which forestalls him. When he is thrown back on himself he understands in his blindness that his uncleanness is out of keeping with its purity. And if he loves he takes pleasure in weeping, neither is it without much groaning that he is forced to return to himself.[56]

299. We are wholly unequal to the task of conceiving this reality, but he whom we love forgives us, he of whom we confess we can neither speak nor think worthily. And yet we are stimulated and drawn on by his love or the love of his love to speak and to think of him.

300. It is for one who entertains such thoughts to abase himself in everything and to glorify in himself the Lord his God, to become of no worth in his own eyes as he contemplates God, to subject himself to every human being for the love of his Creator, to offer up his body as a holy victim, living, pleasing to God, the worship due from him as a rational creature.[57] But before everything he should not think highly of himself, beyond his just estimation but have a sober esteem of himself, according to the measure of faith which God has apportioned to him.[58] He should not entrust his treasures to men's mouths but conceal them in his cell and hide them away in his conscience, so as to have this inscription always in the forefront of his conscience and on the front of his cell: "My secret is my own, my secret is my own."[59]

THE END OF DOM WILLIAM'S EPISTLE TO THE BRETHREN OF MONT DIEU

53. Ex 33:20.   54. Mk 12:30.   55. Mk 12:31; Lev 19:18.

56. There are many parallels to this passage in the writings of William of St Thierry; see for example Exp 146.

57. Rom 12:1.   58. Rom 12:3.   59. Is 24:16.

SELECTED BIBLIOGRAPHY

Sources

——*Vita antiqua,* ed. A. Poncelet in *Mélanges Godefroid Kurth,* vol. 1 (Liège, 1908), pp. 85–96.

William of St Thierry, *Enigma of Faith,* ed. J. P. Migne (Paris, 1902) PL 180:397–440 (Cistercian Fathers Series 9).

——*Exposition on the Song of Songs,* ed. J. M. Déchanet, Sources Chrétiennes 82 (Paris: Cerf, 1962) (Cistercian Fathers Series 6).

——*The Golden Epistle:*

Davy, M. M., *Un traité de la Vie solitaire, Epistola ad Fratres de Monte Dei, de Guillaume de Saint-Thierry* (Paris: Vrin, 1940).

Mabillon, J., *Sti Bernardi abbatis primi Clarae-vallensis Opera omnia* (Paris, 1667, 1690) vol. 2, cols. 199–232.

Migne, J. P., in *S. Bernardi opera omnia,* vol. 3 (Paris, 1862) PL 184:307–364.

Thomas, R., *Lettre aux Frères du Mont-Dieu,* 2 vols., text, introduction, French trans., notes, Pain de Cîteaux 33–34 (Chambarand, 1968).

Tissier, B., *Bibliotheca Patrum Cisterciensium,* vol. 4 (Bonnefontaine, 1662).

——*Life of Saint Bernard,* ed., J. P. Migne, in *S. Bernardi opera omnia,* vol. 4, PL 185:225–268.

——*Meditations,* ed., R. Thomas, *Oraisons Méditées,* 2 vols., text, introduction, French trans., notes, Pain de Cîteaux 21–22 (Chambarand, 1964) (Cistercian Fathers Series 3).

——*Mirror of Faith,* ed. J. M. Déchanet, *Le Mirroir de la Foi,* text, introduction, French trans., notes, Bibliothèque de Spiritualité Médiévale (Bruges: Beyaert, 1946) (Cistercian Fathers Series 9).

——*The Nature and Dignity of Love,* ed. R. Thomas, *Nature et dignité de l'amour,* text, introduction, French trans., notes, Pain de Cîteaux 24 (Chambarand, 1965) (Cistercian Fathers Series 15).

——*The Nature of Body and Soul,* ed. J. P. Migne (Paris, 1902) PL 180:695–726 (Cistercian Fathers Series 24).

——*On Contemplating God,* ed. J. Hourlier, *La Contemplation de Dieu,* Sources Chrétiennes 61 (Paris: Cerf, 1959) (Cistercian Fathers Series 3).

——*Prayer, Ibid.*

Translations

Davy, M. M., *Un traité de la Vie solitaire, Epistola ad Fratres de Monte Dei, de Guillaume de Saint-Thierry* (Paris: Vrin, 1946).

Déchanet, J. M., *Lettre d'Or aux Frères du Mont-Dieu* (Paris: Descleé, 1956).

McCann, J. and Shewring, W., *The Golden Epistle of Abbot William of St Thierry* (London: Sheed and Ward, 1930).

Ravelet, A., *Oeuvres de Saint Bernard,* vol. 4 (Paris, 1868).

Studies

Adam, A., *Guillaume de Saint-Thierry, sa vie et ses oeuvres* (Bourg, 1923).

Bouyer, L., *The Cistercian Heritage,* trans. E. Livingston (Westminster, Md.: Newman, 1958).

Davy, M. M., "Ascèse et vertu selon Guillaume de Saint-Thierry" in *Revue d'ascétique et de mystique,* 19 (1938) pp. 225–244.

——"La théologie spirituelle de la Lettre d'Or" in *Vie Spirituelle,* 53 (1937) supplément, pp. 86–115.

——"Les trois étapes de la vie spirituelle" in *Recherches de science religieuse,* 23 (1933) pp. 569–588.

Déchanet, J. M., "A propos de la Lettre aux Frères du Mont-Dieu" in *Collectanea O.C.R.,* 5 (1938) pp. 3–8, 81–95.

——"Autour d'une querelle fameuse, de l'Apologie à la Lettre d'Or" in *Revue d'ascétique et de mystique,* 20 (1939) pp. 3–34.

——"Aux sources de la doctrine spirituelle de Guillaume de Saint-Thierry" in *Collectanea O.C.R.,* 5 (1938–39) pp. 187–198, 262–278.

——*Aux sources de la spiritualité de Guillaume de Saint-Thierry* (Bruges: Beyaert, 1940).

——*William of St Thierry, the Man and his Works,* trans. R. Strachan (Cistercian Studies Series 10).

Elder, E. R., "The Way of Ascent: the Meaning of Love in the Thought of William of Saint Thierry" in *Studies in Medieval Culture,* vol. 1, ed. J. R. Sommerfeldt (Kalamazoo: Western Michigan University, 1964) pp. 39–47.

Fiske, A., "William of St. Thierry and Friendship" in *Cîteaux*, 12 (1961) pp. 5–27.

Gilson, E., *The Mystical Theology of Saint Bernard*, trans. A. Downes (New York: Sheed and Ward, 1940).

Le Bail, A., "La spiritualité cistercienne, Guillaume de Saint-Thierry" in *Cahiers du cercle thomiste*, 2 (Paris, 1927) pp. 396–402.

Ryan, P., "The Witness of William of St Thierry to the Spirit and Aims of the Early Cistercians" in *The Cistercian Spirit: A Symposium*, ed. M. B. Pennington (Cistercian Studies Series 3) pp. 224–253.

Thomas, R., *Notes sur Guillaume de Saint-Thierry*, 4 vols., Pain de Cîteaux 1–4 (Chambarand, 1959).

Walsh, J., "William of Saint Thierry and Spiritual Meanings" in *Revue d'ascétique et de mystique*, 35 (1959) pp. 27–42.

Wilmart, A., "Les écrits spirituels des deux Guigues, la Lettre aux Frères du Mont-Dieu" in *Revue Mabillon*, 5 (1924) pp. 127–158.

——"La préface de la Lettre aux Frères du Mont-Dieu" in *Revue Bénédictine*, 36 (1924) pp. 229–247.

——"La série et la date des ouvrages de Guillaume de Saint-Thierry" in *Revue Mabillon*, 14 (1924) pp. 156–167.

ANALYTIC INDEX

The references are to the paragraphs in *The Golden Epistle;* those in italics refer to the *Prefatory Letter.*

Chastity, 60, 187, 188, 214, 252, 264.
Christ, 9, 11, 19, 39, 72, 115, 162f,
  232.
  became man that we might be
    like God, 272.
  example of poverty, 160.
  leadership, 8.
  mediator, 174.
  meditation on, 171, 174.
  members of his body, 119.
  see also Passion of our Lord.
Church, 9, 11.
  primitive, 162.
Cicero, 30 (note 69).
City of God, 13.
City of refuge, 143.
Common good, must take preced-
    ence over personal satisfaction,
    12.
Common life, 162, 190.
Common observance, 75f, 78, 106,
  109.
Communion, spiritual, 115ff.
Compassion, 146.
Compunction, 30, 99.
Concupiscence, 236.
Conscience, 56, 61f, 101, 106, 216,
  286, 300.
  daily examination of, 254.
  inner cell, *q. v.*, 105.
Constancy, 37.
Contemplation, 18, 189, 195, 203,
    209, 249, 274, 277, 297, 300.
  relation to activity, 18.
  see also Enjoyment of God.
Contemplative life, 278.
Contrition, 86.
Conversion, *see* Monastic conversion
Curiosity, 66, 70, 188, 216, 236.

Daily Examine, 108.
David (King), *3*, 121.
  Prophet, 110.
  Psalmist, 177.
Desert, the, 13, 70, 158.
Desire, basic, 256.
Detachment, 251.

Devotion, 31f, 86, 101, 117, 272.
  examples of, 3.
  see also Holy Spirit, Piety.
Dignity of man, 212.
Dilection, 235, 256f.
Discretion, 54, 126, 229.
  not in the beginner, 53.
  to love God without any limit, 230.
Disobedience, 116, 223, 240.
  examples of, 54.
Distractions, 62ff, 246, 255.
Divine Office, 83, 111f, 114.
  see also Vigils.

Egypt, 1, 157.
Ehud, 18.
Elijah, 12.
Enigma of Faith, summary of the
    grounds of the formulations of
    faith, *7f, 12.*
Enjoyment of God, 31f.
Eternity, God's, 277.
Example, good, 103, 193.
Experience of God, 268f.
Exposition of the Song of Songs, 9.
Eucharist, 118.
  see also Communion.
Ezekiel the Prophet, 73.

Face of God, 25f, 165, 195, 268, 297.
  makes man realize his imperfection,
    271.
  see also Vision of God.
Faith, *4f*, 60, 119, 167, 170, 174, 177,
    207, 252, 267, 275, 279, 281,
    286, 293, 300.
  becomes a movement of love, 175.
Fasting, 214.
Fasts, 86, 126.
Father (God), 6, 181f, 186, 263.
Fathers of Religious Institutes, role
    of, 22.
Fear, 272.
  of God, 51.
  of the Lord, 124.
Folly, 48, 54, 89, 124, 143.
Fools for God's sake, 8.
Fortitude, 51, 227.

Novices, *2, 6, 9*, 68, 78.
Epistle written for them, *2*.
lacking discretion, 68.
"prudent," 54.
see also Animal man.

Obedience, 44, 51ff, 68, 75f, 94, 97f,
101, 138, 191, 227, 229, 231.
a trusty guardian of the will,
whether it be obedience to a
command or to advice, whether
it involve subordination or be
prompted by charity alone, 240.
of charity, 240.
of necessity, 240.
perfect obedience, 190.
Observances, 66.
see also Common observance.
Obstinacy, 37.
Office, *see* Divine Office.
On Contemplating God, 9.
On the Epistle to the Romans, 10.
On the Nature and Dignity of Love, 9.
On the Nature of the Body, 13.
On the Nature of the Soul, 13.
On the Sacrament of the Altar, 9.
Openness, 98.
Opus Dei, see Divine Office.

Passion, 272.
meditation on, 115.
Passion of our Lord, 13.
Patience, 60, 76, 146, 183, 214, 227,
252.
Paul of Egypt, 13.
Paul the Apostle (St), *15*, 19, 26ff,
39f, 48, 70, 90, 104, 113, 121,
127, 130, 141, 161ff, 167, 180f,
214f, 252, 264, 278.
Paul the Hermit (St), 13.
Peace, *15*, 24, 29, 60, 177, 213, 216,
252.
Penance, 78.
see also Mortification.
Perfect, the, 216.
Perfection, 15f, 39, 141, 249ff, 276,
287, 300.

consists in this life of forgetting
what lies behind and pressing
on, 40.
each state has a measure proper to
itself, 44.
our Lord's summation of it, 288.
to refuse to be perfect is to be at
fault, 259.
see also Likeness to God.
Perseverance, 94.
Peter (St), 12, 142, 240.
Philosophers of this world, 7.
Piety, 11, 24, 27f, 37, 60, 115, 119,
171, 192, 212, 279.
definition of, 27.
the worship of God, 26.
Pluralism, 23.
communal, 38.
personal, 39, 41.
Poverty, 9, 76, 94, 147ff, 153, 157f,
214.
of Christ, 272.
spiritual, 194.
see also Christ.
Poverty of spirit, 13, 146, 175, 192,
216.
Prayer, 32, 35, 64, 110ff, 123, 169ff,
249.
kinds of:
petitions, 177, 182.
prayer, 179.
supplications, 178f, 183.
thanksgiving, 180f.
should interrupt reading, 123.
unceasing, 181.
Presence of God, 102.
Presumption, 223.
Pride, 17, 37, 48, 59, 143, 223, 236.
Priesthood,
ministerial, 117.
of the laity, 117.
Prophets, 11.
see also David, Elijah, Ezekiel,
Isaiah, Jeremiah.
Prudence, 143, 227.
carnal, 48.
true, 51.

CISTERCIAN PUBLICATIONS

THE CISTERCIAN FATHERS SERIES

THE WORKS OF BERNARD OF CLAIRVAUX

Treatises I (*Apologia* to Abbot William, On Precept and Dispensation) CF 1

On the Song of Songs I CF 4

Treatises II (The Steps of Humility, On Loving God) CF 13

Five Books on Consideration CF 37

THE WORKS OF WILLIAM OF ST THIERRY

On Contemplating God, Prayer, Meditations CF 3

Exposition on the Song of Songs CF 6

The Enigma of Faith CF 9

The Golden Epistle CF 12

THE WORKS OF AELRED OF RIEVAULX

Treatises I (On Jesus at the Age of Twelve, Rule for a Recluse, The Pastoral Prayer) CF 2

Spiritual Friendship CF 5

THE WORKS OF GUERRIC OF IGNY

Liturgical Sermons
two volumes CF 8, CF 32

THE CISTERCIAN STUDIES SERIES

CISTERCIAN STUDIES

The Cistercian Spirit: A Symposium in Memory of Thomas Merton CS 3

The Eleventh-century Background of Citeaux by Bede Lackner CS 8

Studies in Medieval Cistercian History, edited Joseph F. O'Callahan CS 13

Contemporary Community edited M. Basil Pennington CS 21

Bernard of Clairvaux: Studies Presented to Dom Jean Leclercq CS 23

William of St Thierry: The Man and His Work by J. M. Dechanet CS 10

Thomas Merton: The Man and His Work by Dennis Q. McInerny CS 27

Cistercian Sign Language by Robert Barakat CS 11

MONASTIC TEXTS AND STUDIES

The Climate of Monastic Prayer by Thomas Merton CS 1

Evagrius Ponticus: Praktikos and Chapter on Prayer CS 4

The Abbot in Monastic Tradition by Pierre Salmon CS 14

Why Monks? by Francois Vandenbroucke CS 17

Silence: Silence in the Rule of St Benedict by Ambrose Wathen CS 22

The Sayings of the Desert Fathers tr Benedicta Ward CS 59

One Yet Two: Monastic Tradition East and West CS 29